à faire de [...] ...tend
nous classerons les lettres après, de façon
à [ce] que jamais la réponse de suive
la lettre. Je demanderai après
à changer [...] d'Alériones.
Dans une nouvelle que je viens de
finir M[.] de Brayes est déjà
[...] d'Alérione [...] point[.]
1re confusion désobligeante
de M[.] de Brayes,

Ton ami bien dévoué
J. [Marfelberg]

Paris lundi 9 [...] [...] herbes jusqu'à
lundi matin et même après avec

OTHER
PEOPLE'S
LETTERS

A Memoir

Also by Mina Curtiss

The Midst of Life: *A Romance*
Bizet and His World
A Forgotten Empress: *Anna Ivanovna and Her Era,*
1730–1740

EDITOR AND TRANSLATOR

Letters of Marcel Proust
My Friend Degas *by Daniel Halévy*

EDITOR

Olive, Cypress and Palm: *An Anthology of Love and Death*
Letters Home

OTHER
PEOPLE'S
LETTERS

A Memoir

by

Mina Curtiss

Illustrated with Photographs

ISBN: 0 333 24255 6

First published in the United States of America 1978 by
Houghton Mifflin Company

First published in Great Britain 1978 by

MACMILLAN LONDON LIMITED
4 Little Essex Street London WC2R 3LF
and Basingstoke
Associated Companies in Delhi, Dublin,
Hong Kong, Johannesburg, Lagos, Melbourne,
New York, Singapore and Tokyo

Copyright © 1978 by Mina Curtiss

*To Jenny Bradley,
humbly, and with love*

Acknowledgments

I AM INDEBTED to Mme. Suzy Mante-Proust, Proust's niece and heir, and to Mme. Louis Joxe, Daniel Halévy's daughter, for permission to print the unpublished fragment in the appendix of this book; also to Mrs. Simon Hodgson, daughter of Prince Antoine Bibesco, for permission to quote from his unpublished writings.

I also wish to thank the Duc and the Comte de Gramont for their kindness in giving me a choice of pictures of their grandmother, the Comtesse Greffulhe and their aunt, the Duchesse de Clermont-Tonnerre.

I am grateful to Mme. Liliane Ziegel for correcting the mistakes in my copy of the original manuscript of Proust's letters as well as supplying me with several of the illustrations in this book. My former secretary, Elenor Fardig, typed many drafts of much of the manuscript with patience and accuracy. Her successor, Lynne Robbins, has been equally meticulous in typing the final chapters.

Parts of chapters five and ten were published in *The Cornhill,* No. 982, Spring 1950, in an article entitled "Céleste." Some of chapter fifteen appeared in the preface to my translation of Daniel Halévy's *Degas Parle,* entitled *My Friend Degas,* published in 1966 by the Wesleyan University Press.

Preface

THE NOTION that *Research and Detection* could be a suitable subtitle for this book occurred to me as I read through
the finished manuscript. But research can be a formidable word
with a wide variety of connotations, many of which might dis-
courage readers, an effect no author would choose to risk.

My earliest conception of research while I was an undergraduate was limited to the realm of academia — faculty scholarship,
Ph.D.'s, remote from what I then regarded as life. After gradu-
ation in the summer of 1918, I discovered that by passing a
seven-hour written examination given in the Boston Custom
House Tower I could become a "Research Clerk" in M.I.5. The
very idea of working in Military Intelligence, even on a somewhat nondescript level, seemed both exciting and patriotic. I
could hardly have imagined then that at the end of the war in
November my work would consist of mapping out routes for our
army to invade Russia through Poland, that unfortunate country
having already been ravaged and occupied by the Germans. My
sources were a 1904 and a 1912 Baedeker stamped "Secret." At
the end of each day I was required to hand them over to a major
who locked them into a vault.

Since then research, although it may still retain a certain mystique of intellectual prestige, an aura of mystery, has become a widely known form of activity, with definite associations in the public mind: "pure" research — Einstein, the atom bomb; research and development — the "military-industrial complex"; consumer or market research — invasion of privacy of anyone listed in the telephone directory.

Curiosity, a search for clues, is, of course, the basic impetus behind all research. It is a form of detection, although I suspect that very few members of the academic profession would choose to place themselves in the same category as sleuths in whodunits. Not so me. Admittedly, when I started this book I did not conceive of its bearing any relation to my nightly insomniac reading of nonviolent suspense stories. But now that I have read the finished work I find myself identifying more easily with Miss Marple and Miss Silver, those deceptively naive lady detectives, than with the scholars who analyze the work of Marcel Proust. Yet it was translating his letters that set me off on the adventures described in this book.

One day, after I had been working on the translation for two or three years, it suddenly occurred to me that these correspondents were not just names or literary figures but living people whom, if I went to France, I could meet and get to know; people who could supply me with information about the great novelist, unavailable in books. So I went. I met many of Proust's friends, and this book is an account of a rather special form of research, neither literary nor academic, but human, personal, social, and even sociological, an unpredictable experience that I can now see was a turning point in my life as a writer.

October 13, 1977
Weston, Connecticut

Illustrations

(Following page 116)

Marcel Proust, 1891 sketch by Jacques-Emile Blanche;
Copyright © by S.P.A.D.E.M., Paris, 1978
(Bibliothèque Nationale)

Proust, 1892 drawing by Paul Baignères.

The Duchesse de Clermont-Tonnerre, portrait by Laszlo.

Mme. Marie Scheikévitch.

Geneviève Halévy Bizet Straus.

Jenny Bradley. *(Courtesy of Mme. Bradley)*

The author in 1955.

Mme. Céleste Albaret.

Céleste and Odilon Albaret. *(Courtesy of Mme. Albaret)*

The Albarets' Hôtel d'Alsace et Lorraine.

Céleste Albaret's present residence.

Prince Antoine Bibesco.

Bibesco residence on the Ile St.-Louis.

Letter from Proust to Bibesco.

PART
ONE

Chapter 1

FEMME DE LETTRES, if it had an English synonym, would most accurately describe my profession. For letters have literally been the driving force behind every book I have produced. A passion, only recently outworn, for reading other people's letters stems from a traumatic episode in my childhood, the catalytic significance of which penetrated only some forty years later.

When I was seven or eight years old, one rainy afternoon on my governess' day off I managed to escape surveillance and invade the forbidden territory of the attic. The wickedness of this insubordination was augmented by the fact that I had on a brand-new dress, supposedly reserved for wear on the train to visit Atlantic City, where my grandparents always spent the Easter holidays. Why I was permitted to wear it that particular day I can't remember, but the dress itself I can still visualize perfectly. Navy blue serge with a pleated skirt, it had a jumper blouse trimmed with suspenderlike strips of navy blue and white polka dot foulard. Worn over a white batiste guimpe, it was not the ideal costume for exploring an attic filled with long-undusted trunks.

The first one I opened, because it was the smallest, contained dozens of ribbon-tied packets of letters — mother's and father's, written during their three-year-long engagement when he was in disfavor with her family. I recognized my father's handwriting on an envelope addressed to mother's maiden name at a hotel in Mount Clemens, Michigan, and started to untie the ribbon around the package when without warning mother swooped down upon me and snatched the unread letters from my hand. I was not unfamiliar with her tantrums. But the rage she let loose at what she apparently regarded as an unforgivable invasion of privacy could not have been more violent had I sneaked into Paradise and caught Adam and Eve committing the pre-original sin. She took all the letters and burned them. The incident was never again mentioned. I wasn't even scolded for getting dust on my new unlaunderable dress. Nevertheless, I was permeated with guilt, shame, and most of all curiosity as to the significance of my sin.

From that time forth I was convinced that the clue to the secret of life, the creative process, lay in personal letters intended for somebody else. As a result of this uncontrollable curiosity I developed the habit of reading any letters I came across. I was quite honest about it. I warned friends, roommates in college, guests in my house against leaving any private papers where I might be tempted to read them. And after fifty years I still blush when I think of an evening soon after our return from our wedding journey to the house where my husband had lived with his first wife. Poking around his desk one day I found and read letters she had written him years before. As he walked in the door that evening I confessed my sin in tears of guilt and jealousy. But the sin turned out to be almost worth committing because he gallantly took the blame for it. "You warned me," he said. "I should have destroyed them. I just forgot all about it."

Letters I wrote to him in 1933, five summers after he died, formed my first published book. From June through September each day I would write to him about the continuing things, the daily events at our farm in Ashfield, Massachusetts, that seemed only half real without his sharing them. How the garden grew, the welfare of the cows and horses, the adventures of the cats and dogs he knew, and the character of new acquisitions; important dates like the first cutting of the hay, the first peas from the garden. And there were conversations, too, with the farmer and the gardener, the lady who churned the butter, the wonderful blacksmith who assured me that people didn't speak of me as "the widow Curtiss," a label I couldn't face. They were frivolous letters, I suppose, inasmuch as there was nothing burdensome or anxious in them, nothing to disturb the peace of the vague, undefinable world of eternal values where I presumed his essence must be.

When the frost came, before I left for winter in the city, I read over the letters for the first time. "It's a book," I thought. "It should be published for people like me who like to read other people's letters." So with no second thoughts I drove to Boston — only a few hours from Ashfield — and barged into the office of *The Atlantic Monthly*. The formidable Ellery Sedgwick was not a person one called on without an appointment. But he liked my father, Louis Kirstein, and my brother Lincoln, and was not himself averse to a good-looking woman. So he received me. I told him I had just finished a book that I thought should run serially in *The Atlantic*.

"But we don't run serials."

"You used to," I said.

"Not for a long time . . . What is this book about?"

"It's letters to a dead man."

He looked at me as though I were mad. "How can you write letters to a dead man?"

"Read them and see," I said, plunked the typescript down on his desk, and departed.

Three days later he telephoned me to say that the book would appear in four parts, the first having already gone to press. No precedent to subsequent years of struggle with publishers could have been more deceptive. For with rare exceptions I have found publishers the enemy — victims of unavoidable hypocrisy, induced by the conflict between encouraging authors to write "good" books that may not sell and making as much money as possible themselves off any books that will.

My next book of letters grew out of the war. When I observed how little attention the country and small-town people around me paid to propaganda broadcasts from Washington or New York, it occurred to me that a local point of view, drawing on familiar people and places, would be far more likely to attract and hold their interest. So I hied me to Washington, where I found great difficulty in achieving an appointment with the head of the propaganda office. Although he was an old and intimate friend, he received me politely, as though I were someone who had come with a letter of introduction from some official personage.

I told him my theory about the importance of grass-roots radio programs and said I would like to try writing some radio scripts for my district, Franklin County, Massachusetts, to serve possibly as pilot programs for the Middle West. Such trivia didn't interest him. He offered me a job selling bonds in factories. However, he did say one relevant thing. "What do you know about the Middle West?" This question, which was rather like the minor operation of having your eyelids lifted to improve your vision, opened up a whole new point of view.

Confronted with the fact that indeed I knew nothing about the Middle West, I bought four WPA guidebooks, those splendidly useful products of the 1930s Depression — Wisconsin, Missouri, North Dakota, and Iowa. I was seduced by Iowa, the state with the highest literacy rate in the nation and the fourth-largest representation in the navy. So during my Easter vacation from Smith College where I was then teaching, I spent three weeks in Cedar Rapids, Iowa, a city as attractive as the guidebook description.

I chose it because Louis Sullivan was the architect of its municipal island and because Grant Wood had not only made the stained-glass windows in the city hall but there was a museum devoted to his work. I went there alone with only two letters of introduction — one I had coaxed out of the editor of the newspaper *PM*, appointing me in rather vague terms as its representative. The other was from an old friend, Carl Van Vechten, to his nephew, the president of a bank. During the three weeks I was there I interviewed dozens of men and women on every social level: Junior League ladies, city officials, executives and employees of the colossal Quaker Oats and other factories, the head of the newly organized CIO meat-packers union, and, most helpful of all, Hugh Johnson, the Negro poet, college student, bus boy, who brought me dinner in my room each night. He told me about his family — farmers for generations — and we talked about books and writers: Tom Wolfe, whom I knew, Proust, Dostoevski. Only one person I interviewed was antagonistic — the head of an important war industry who turned out later to have been a Nazi sympathizer or spy.

For the first time in my life I kept a journal. Every night I dictated my day's conversations to the hotel stenographer, who also owned a small radio factory. Then with the journal under my arm I went to Des Moines, hoping that a reading of it would persuade Gardner Cowles, the owner of the *Register and Tribune,* to let me try out a grass-roots program on that paper's radio station. Through whose influence he accorded me a long, patient interview I can't remember — probably some friend of my father's. In any case, after listening to the account of my stay in Cedar Rapids (he didn't read the journal, which remains unread by anyone but me) and after telephoning CBS in New York to verify my statement that I had helped with scripts for Orson Welles's and John Houseman's *Mercury Theatre of the Air,* he accepted my idea. I could come to Des Moines in June, when my teaching term was over, and experiment with one program a week for six weeks. The paper would bear the expense but, of course, I would receive no salary.

In June I went to Des Moines, terrified of what I had undertaken because actually I had never written or produced a whole radio program on my own. But fortunately Dorothy Walker, a more than competent secretary and a former journalist with experience in timing and deadlines, came with me. Even more fortunately, the *Register and Tribune* each day printed a column of letters from soldiers, giving the names and addresses of their families. Again letters became the catalyst for my work.

To talk to the families we drove miles and miles around central and southern Iowa. Just the words "from the *Register and Tribune*" were a magic key. The hospitality, the invitations to stay for dinner, for supper in farmhouses that to my New England eye looked like mansions, the willingness even to come to Des Moines to be interviewed were beyond anything I could have hoped for or imagined.

Iowa made me for the first time feel that there was a real America to justify the emotion of patriotism. The letters of Iowa soldiers stimulated me to make an anthology of enlisted men's letters from all over the United States. (Officers' letters predominate in similar anthologies.) I wrote a letter to two hundred and fifty newspapers asking them to publish a request to families of servicemen to send me their letters. Most of the city papers, as well as many small-town and village weeklies, cooperated. Within weeks I was swamped with contributions. In cartons, in outsized envelopes, in shoe boxes, or just in paper parcels came more hundreds of letters than even I with my obsessive curiosity could digest. But after I sampled one or two out of every batch it became clear that a collection of single letters would not reproduce or re-create the impact of my Iowa experience. I therefore chose thirty-six series of letters written from a man's first day in the service to his latest and sometimes his last. Sixteen states and almost every branch of the armed services were represented.

Letters Home was published on D-day and had a very good notice on the front page of the New York *Herald Tribune* Sunday book section. But the book failed to attract many readers, although excerpts from it continue to be published in textbooks and anthologies. Obviously my great interest in letters intended for someone else is not widely shared. Even I, when the selection was finally made, felt smothered by other people's letters and thought that never again would I want to read any that weren't written to me.

Yet only three years later in a Paris where I knew as few people as I had in Cedar Rapids, I was searching for unpublished letters of Marcel Proust as well as any firsthand information that would throw light on his work and his life.

Chapter 2

THE SUGGESTION that I should translate Proust's letters came from Edmund Wilson. As early as 1930, when I had just finished my first reading of *A la recherche du temps perdu,* he expressed an opinion on Proust as man and as novelist that continues to coincide with my own. "... The little man with the great eyes, the Saracen's beak and the ill-fitting dress shirt, still dominates his and our own special contemporary world; he has supplied symbols in terms of which we see it and in the light of which we may better understand it. Let us not wonder, and let us not complain, if he suffered from its most insidious diseases."

Following the advice of that irreplaceable critic, the only true American *homme de lettres* of my generation, led me into an unpredictable exploration of that world. The first step was reading for a year all Proust's published letters, collected and uncollected, searching for the unpublished and learning to decipher that formidably variable handwriting. My aim was to choose the letters that revealed most clearly the functioning of the process that created his novel. Concentration on this literary idea — nearly three years of translating and re-translating, often as many as eight drafts of a single letter — apparently blinded me to the fact that the correspondents were human beings, not merely links in the chain of Proust's development as a novelist. Then one day I had a revelation. These correspondents, these *Chers amis* and *Chères amies,* these *Monsieurs* and *Madames* were not just characters in the book I was, after a fashion, composing. They were living people whom I could meet if I just went to France and found them. The things they could tell me would give life to my book, transform academic notes into firsthand information. So I decided to go to Paris as soon as possible. The procedure was not simple in 1947.

To reach Paris one had to go via London, Dover, and Calais. Large ships could not dock at Cherbourg, still unrestored from war damage. England, however, was struggling through such a severe food and power shortage that only persons with essential business could enter. To secure a visa two letters from British citizens confirming the validity of one's claim were necessary. My sponsors were David Garnett and Harold Nicolson.

Afterthought, 1977

When friends who read the manuscript of this book said that I would have to identify David Garnett as his writing is unknown to younger generations, I was sure they must be mistaken. But they weren't. The editors of a 1976 issue of *The New Statesman,* in order to clarify the significance of the title to his review of Virginia Woolf's *Moments of Being* — "Lady into Woolf" — identified him as follows in their contributor's column: "David Garnett was closely associated with the Bloomsbury group. One of his early novels, *Lady into Fox,* was published in 1922. His most recent book, *Plough over the Bones,* came out in 1973."

But *Lady into Fox* was not just "one of his early novels." It was his first novel and was awarded both the Hawthornden and the James Tait Black Memorial prizes for the most original novel of the year. In the last three years he has published *The Master Cat* and *Up She Rises,* a fictionalized biography of his great-grandmother.

David grew up literary, so to speak. He is the son of Constance, the best-known translator of Russian literature, and of Edward, the noted editor and friend of Joseph Conrad, of both D. H. and T. E. Lawrence, of H. E. Bates and Henry Green. More original than either of his parents, David has written a dozen or more novels, a unique biography of Pocahontas, and a three-volume autobiography. In 1922, when I first met him, a prophecy that he would have dwindled for today's reading public into a recurrent but seemingly minor figure in the Bloomsbury saga would have been unbelievable. Byron was indeed right when he wrote:

> What is the end of fame? 'Tis but to fill
> A certain portion of uncertain paper.

Today, I am afraid, in this country at least, David is best known as the editor of letters, most recently those of a woman who in her youth impressed me as a permanently adolescent, gamine-type of dabbler in the arts — Dora Carrington. Her letters reveal her to have been a femme fatale even more havoc-wreaking than her contemporary, that overpowering great lady, Ottoline Morrell.

Although Bloomsbury, that exclusive circle to which David introduced me, differed vastly in the aims, the quality, and the mystique of its membership from the eighteenth-century "Hell-Fire Club," it might well have shared its motto: "Do what you will." Impressed as I then was by their talent and/or genius, I suppose I should logically feel impelled to add my two cents' worth to the history of the legendary group. But it would be distasteful to me to add even my fringy impressions to the prevalent flood of detailed reminiscences and letters. Grateful that in my innocent youth I was unaware of the intriguing web of recently revealed personal relations between all the "Bloomsberries" I met, it would be supererogatory to recount my uninformed brief encounters with Virginia Woolf, Morgan Forster, Maynard Keynes, and Lytton Strachey.

Sharply etched in my memory though these notables are, I am not tempted to write about their now-famous microcosm into which I was received with courteous curiosity, a welcome I imagine not unlike that given the American "noble savage" by eighteenth-century literati. Overawed by it then, somewhat repelled by its present overexposure —who slept with whom and when, psychological incest on a grand scale — I find that I remember most happily the non-Bloomsbury side of more than half a century of friendship with "Bunny" Garnett, whom I alone have always called by his given name, David.

His and my recollections of our first meeting do not exactly jibe. In a charming pamphlet — *Never Be a Bookseller* — he wrote in 1929, "One beautiful dark American girl refused my book with unusual vigor — and came back to ask for it next day. That was the origin of the most valued friendship that book brought me, and it brought many friends." His recollection, however, was incorrect, subject perhaps to a certain male vanity. I didn't go back the next day. He sent me the book. How I happened to go to his book shop in the first place I don't think he ever knew.

In London from June 1922 to August 1923 on leave of absence from my job as English instructor at Smith College, I attended classes at London University and was psychoanalyzed by Ernest Jones. On the way home from Eileen Power's brilliant lectures, "Medieval People," I shared a bus seat with a fellow student — a romantically handsome young man called Raisley Moorsom, who I kept hoping would one day ask me to tea. Eventually he did. But in the meantime he talked a great deal about his brilliant, witty friend, Francis Birrell, whom I must meet. He ran a book shop at 30 Gerrard Street, and I could go there any day and talk to him. So I went, and found another tall, handsome, blond, blue-eyed young man who I assumed was Birrell.

I told him I wanted to send books home for Christmas presents, but didn't know what to choose. There was a new Huxley not yet published in America, he said. "Posthumous?" I asked. "*Aldous* Huxley," he replied, and handed me *Mortal Coils*. The only Huxley with whom I was familiar was Aldous' grandfather, Thomas Henry, some of whose essays were required reading in the Freshman English class I taught. Until forty years later, when David published his memoirs, I always thought it was my cultural naiveté that had made him fall in love with me. But apparently I was mistaken. In any case, he found a number of suitable books for me to send off. Just as I was leaving the shop he picked up a copy of *Lady into Fox* and showed it to me.

"You are Francis Birrell, aren't you?" I blurted out.

"No, I'm David Garnett."

"If I'd known that I would have bought your book," I said, and fled, overcome with embarrassment, never expecting to see him again.

But I did see him again, many times, after he sent me a copy of the book.

Our relationship, from his point of view, had certain limitations. He could not understand my puritanism, as he called it. And wishing to appear sophisticated, I couldn't explain that one of his first letters shocked me profoundly. It left me with no possible evasion of the difference between Bloomsbury's pragmatic concept of all personal relationships and my deeply ingrained belief in the sanctity of marriage. In my innocence I assumed that no married man could express the feelings he did in the beginning of a letter that concluded casually with the question "Did I tell you that my wife presented me with a most delightful boy about a week ago? He is a very lovely creature with a perfect complexion and I think rather a philosophic disposition. Both he and Ray are in excellent health. I should like you to meet her some day."

If the shock of discovering that he was both husband and father in no way hindered the increasing intensity of our relationship, it remained uncomfortably platonic in spite of both our efforts to overcome my scruples. His idea of love, at least at that time, is expressed in a letter he wrote after we had known each other a few months:

> I shall not say anything to you about love. It's much more simple than that. You make me happy. I am happy when I am with you and when I am not I think about you and that makes me happy. Happiness has probably nothing to do with love, but it is the most important thing and all I want to tell you is how happy I am. You are making me lead an idle life. All I can think of is the pleasure I shall have coming to tea with you, how much I want to go walking with you — and swimming and sailing. How jolly it would be to get under the strawberry nets with you and eat strawberries and so forth — This is a silly letter to write. Tomorrow I'll be reasonable and begin reading Cobbett's English Grammar.

Publishing this letter, after so many years, causes me a slight sense of invasion of privacy, both David's and mine. But since his memoirs are replete with far more intimate descriptions of his various loves, I have overcome my hesitation. For this letter seems to me an illuminating example of Bloomsbury's hedonistic concept of love — highly subjective. As forms of pleasurable exercise I associated walking and swimming with my long-past summers at a girls' camp. Sailing in small boats I have always found both uncomfortable and frightening. And the joys of a strawberry bed I learned only some years later when I married and acquired a garden. But my husband and I always lifted the cheesecloth nets to pick the berries. The idea of happiness that David then thought "the most important thing . . . much more simple than love" now seems like euphoric, youthful nonsense. No love, not even long-tested and enduring love, is ever simple. Happiness can only be incidental. As I look back on a long life, true happiness in contrast to fleeting amusement seems to me to have grown of its own accord out of satisfying work or fulfilled companionship. Pursued and caught like a butterfly it is apt to be as short-lived.

David's fantasy of me as the athletic, amenable girl he wishfully conceived was far less typical of him than the anthropomorphism of the first letter he wrote me after I left England — Lady into Bird. "I love you very much but you are already in these few days as strange to me as a rare hoopoe that after settling on the fence in the backyard and shaking her gilded crest of scarlet tassels suddenly flies over a high tree and is gone forever. So I have been saying to myself I shall never see that lovely rare creature again — what strange vagary can have brought her as a migrant to my door . . ." Migrant I was indeed. But roots I soon found.

Within a year after my return to the United States I met my husband, Henry Tomlinson Curtiss, and not until 1932, four years after his death, did I see David again. This time he came to my door — himself a very special kind of migrant. Deeply depressed over the deaths of his friend Garrow Tomlin in a plane accident, of Lytton Strachey, and the subsequent suicide of Carrington, he was unable to concentrate on his work in progress, a biography of Pocahontas. His letters had been replete with questions about Virginia, and when he asked me about "wild grapevines the size of a man's thigh," I thought he had better come over and verify their dimensions himself. So he and I, with my brother Lincoln and Taylor Hardin, a handsome fox-hunting Virginian, a highly conscious anachronism from the eighteenth century, set out in two cars to search for the site of Powhatan's house, the Chickahominy, and the Pamunkey Indians.

It was a fantastic tour. David has included his version of it in *The Familiar Faces,* Volume III of his memoir, *The Golden Echo.* Inevitably he omitted certain ironic aspects of which only a native could have been aware. Suffice it to say that our historical interests were discrepant. David was preoccupied with his own subject to such an extent that he ruled out our calling his attention to any events after 1617, the year Pocahontas died. My experience of the handicaps in writing biography started only a decade later. So I found his dogmatic ignoring of all post-Pocahontas history irritating. Now I know that of all the blockages a biographer encounters none is more frustrating than would-be helpful contributions about, say, Catherine the Great, whose reign began in 1762, when the Empress Anna Ivanovna, who is one's subject, died in 1740.

My brother's chief interest, which I shared, was the Civil War. But my strongest enthusiasm was for Mr. Jefferson, as he is still called in Charlottesville where I spent the previous winter. It soon became obvious that as Lincoln's and my interest in Pocahontas dwindled rather rapidly it would be wiser for the four of us not to change driving partners each day as we had planned.

David and Taylor progressed together with many stops at the houses of Taylor's hospitable relatives who, David remembered, "replenished our supplies of hard liquor with real white moonshine corn whiskey, made locally." White mule, it was called. I remember it well, burning one's gullet even when disguised as a julep. Glad to forego that indulgence, Lincoln and I arrived in Charlottesville many hours ahead of our companions. Just before midnight there was a beating on the door of my hotel room. David entered in spirits as high as the emanating aroma of whiskey. "Now, my dear," he said, "you may tell me about this Mr. Jefferson of yours."

Motoring with David was always fun, and in the fifties we went on journeys to Italy and through lovely un-tourist-ridden southwest France. There we saw the magical caves of Lascaux, with their prehistoric murals of creatures we could recognize, so superb in design, in color. And we drove past meadows, mauve with autumn crocus in bloom, high up through the Pyrenees to the Cirque de Gavarnie. On muleback we rode up to this spectacular natural amphitheatre, with its snowcapped mountains and massive cascades. Above it too high for us to reach is the Brèche de Roland, a cleft in a wall eighty feet thick which the legendary Roland is said to have hewn with one blow of his sword Durandal, bestowed on him by Charlemagne according to one of the many legends.

The magic we shared in our maturity — prehistoric and legendary — is more memorable to me than the mystique or legend of Bloomsbury, which in the process of becoming history has developed into an industry.

2

Although French has from childhood been my second language, it seemed unlikely that after twenty years' absence from France I would be able to speak at all fluently. The language of Proust's letters, saturated as I was with it, could hardly be adapted to ordinary conversation. (One of the lessons I learned was that while translating enlarges the vocabulary of one's own language it is no aid to proficiency in the foreign tongue.) Practice was obviously essential, and I enjoyed my frequent talking sessions with a charming Harvard instructor, half American, half French, who had been sent to this country as a boy to escape the German occupation. André de Bouchet, who later became a *nouvelle vague* poet, was in 1947 a rather disorderly looking, frighteningly brilliant, shy young man with no particular penchant for Proust. But he had a taste for sweets, and the awe with which his extraordinary intelligence inspired me was lightened by the amount of candy and cookies he devoured while we talked. He had the good sense not to interrupt any flow of speech by correcting my numerous grammatical errors. And he was right. A number of French people I met seemed to derive amusement from my imperfect French. I suppose aliens who speak their language perfectly deprive some natives of a certain sense of superiority. I soon learned that sufficient fluency to avoid interruptions in conversation was far more important than correct speech.

"*Mais vous inventez des mots, Madame,*" Julien Cain, the Director of the Bibliothèque Nationale, once said to me. "*Pourquoi pas, Monsieur?*" I now wish I had had the wit to say, "After all, I am not a member of the French Academy."

Preparing to converse properly with Proust's friends was not the only problem. There was the matter of my appearance. As I was planning to explore his realm, to meet some of the great ladies whose advice he had so meticulously sought about his characters' clothes, it seemed only suitable that I should take as much trouble about my own. So having discovered that that great artist, the couturier Mainbocher, was an ardent Proustian, I put the choice of a wardrobe in his hands.

Being dressed by Mainbocher was like being created by an architect. A papier-mâché figure was constructed so that before and between fittings garments could be carefully draped. After taking into consideration the bitter-cold winter in Europe, the lack of heating in even the best hotels, as well as my budget, we decided on a daytime dress, an evening dress, and the warmest coat in the world. As there is no longer any individual haute couture in this country, and fashionable ladies think nothing of paying thousands of dollars for a dress which they may see duplicated several times at the same gathering, the $5000 cost of my Mainbocher wardrobe now seems rather minimal. In any case, the dividends were rewarding for a far longer time than many less seemingly frivolous investments. The daytime dress was made of black wool, almost as fine as chiffon. Technically it was merely a shirtwaist dress. But designed by Mainbocher, its tailoring the essence of perfection, its only decoration eight brilliant copies of eighteenth-century French diamanté buttons, it made me feel more like a sylph than the amazon I am.

The evening dress, black crepe, was indescribably simple and elegant. It had two belts — one for less formal occasions, a black ribbon with three oval, antique Indian buckles that came off a belt I had got in New Mexico; the other, also a plain black ribbon, but attached to it was a flowing silk drapery in colors blending from pale yellow to bright flame. It had the look of a train but fell down the side of the dress. Wearing it imbued me with a self-confidence I would never otherwise have achieved in strange surroundings. But the masterpiece, the triumph, was the coat which even after a quarter of a century is still a godsend in New England winters. Superficially it resembles in style Proust's famous *pelisse,* which for so many years he wore both indoors and out. But my greatcoat, with its frog fastenings, its "mink-dyed" squirrel lining, now undisguisedly worn squirrel, and its "sable-dyed" mink collar and cuffs, now rubbed shabby, is a creation of expert craftsmanship. It feels weightless. When I looked at Proust's tired, faded *pelisse* in M. Jacques Guerin's remarkable collection of Proustiana, I felt that Marcel would indeed have approved of mine. That bitter-cold spring I not only lived in it by day but often slept in it at night.

3

Clothes, however, occupied minimum space in the big wardrobe trunks, essential for travel in those days but now sold in junky "antique" shops. There was barely room in two of them for a bag of charcoal briquettes, cartons of tinned food, a radio, Kleenex, cigarettes, chocolate bars, crackers, and biscuits. In addition, there was a case of Bourbon whiskey, my briefcase, and typewriter. Thus loaded, I sailed from New York February 19, 1947, on the *Queen Elizabeth.*

Anything less Proustian than the voyage over is hard to imagine. The past seemed indeed permanently lost in the dismal atmosphere pervading the ship. "The help are so weary," I wrote home, "so different from the days when the steward and stewardess used to be one's mama and papa. I literally had to beg the steward to carry my typewriter and another bag off the ship as I could only manage my loaded briefcase and handbag. The stewardess didn't even come and say goodbye to get her tip. I had to look for her. So it isn't money that matters. It's just a terrible inner hopelessness and weariness that is most painful to see."

The gloom was intensified as the ship docked at Southampton early in the morning. For just as we were about to land, some cargo ships also arrived, laden with food, and the dock-workers struck because they quite rightly felt the food ships should be unloaded before the passengers on a luxury liner. Hours passed on the by then unheated ship — dining rooms and bars closed — while negotiations for settling the strike went on. It was settled in a characteristically class-conscious British fashion. A number of Cunard clerical workers volunteered to unload the first-class, while leaving the unhappy cabin and tourist passengers to freeze and starve until the following day.

We eventually got off the ship in midafternoon onto the snow-littered pier. The customs shed was damp and cold. The inspectors' own discomfort increasingly diminished their sense of duty. After shivering with cold, standing for hours in a long queue, my turn came. The inspector looked hopelessly at my dozen or so pieces of luggage and just chalked them off.

"I am on the second boat train to London," I wrote to a friend. "It was supposed to leave at five and left at eight. So far no food is in evidence but there have been rumors of it. It is now nine o'clock. My last meal was breakfast. The train, of course, is unheated, but it's not as cold as I thought it would be. In other words, the suffering of the rich and privileged is not acute. I am wearing woolen underpants, fleece-lined ski shoes, a heavy man's sweater which I bought on board ship, a heavy tweed coat and skirt, a cashmere hooded scarf, a fur-lined coat with a cashmere blanket over my knees which even so feel cold. In the seat next to me is a very charming woman in a state of deep depression. She is a Texan, married to an Englishman, and has lived in this country for twenty years. She has been visiting her mother in America for the first time since the war, and her aversion to coming back is almost frantic. 'Don't let America change,' she kept saying over and over again. 'You're all so alive. Here there's no hope anymore.'"

Along the tracks and as far as one could see there was snow. At home in New England snow is part of nature. But here in "this green and pleasant land" it becomes an intrusive assault. Hardly any lights were lighted as we drew into London. My spirits were very low. But they rose rapidly.

The Berkeley Hotel was actually warm. The welcoming night porter was of the pre-war caretaking school, a personage almost unknown to today's travelers. After apologizing for the lack of electricity he led me up four flights of stairs, grotesquely lighted by railroad-style kerosene lanterns. I hardly dared ask him whether at eleven o'clock at night it would be possible for me to have something to eat, perhaps a sandwich and a pot of tea. But he volunteered to find some supper for me. And at midnight I sat eating gloriously hot canned soup and thinly sliced Spam disguised under a covering of fresh green mustard and cress. That delicious English delicacy, with its tiny white stems and crisp, peppery, dark green leaves, became for a moment a symbol of "this earth, this realm, this England."

Although my Proustian adventures did not start in London, some undefined impulse, perhaps a variation of the sense of participating in live history that I felt in Cedar Rapids, prompted me again to record in a journal the events of each day.

February 26 The most heartwarming thing that could have hap-
    1947   pened to me was David's arrival last night at the

same time as my supper. It was a total surprise. He had come in from the country to meet me and had gone to the station to meet one boat train after another — no proper schedule, of course. In the eleven years since I have seen him his life has changed greatly. His hair is silvery now but his eyes are as shiny blue as ever, his face as ruddy, and his characteristic bear hug heartwarming and rejuvenating. He told me about his new wife, Vanessa's daughter Angelica [Bell], whom he married five years ago, and his two daughters, Amaryllis and Henrietta. He talked, too, about the war work he was most proud of — preventing the intended bombing of the Vilmorin seed beds in France, which would have resulted in a terrible, indefinite food shortage for France.

Today he took me to lunch and then showed me the ruins of London. Forewarned as I was from photographs and reports from people who had been here, the actual impact of this somber, grim, ugly city — once so beautiful — the rows of houseless façades; interiors with strips of wallpaper and damaged furniture visible; the great empty bomb-holes, some still rubble filled, was unbearable. The most macabre thing was all the stopped street clocks. When they were going one never noticed them. It seemed somehow symbolic of the general hopelessness. I couldn't say anything. I just sat next to David and wept as I can't remember ever crying before. It wasn't like a nightmare because it was real. It was snowing again, whitening the piles of dirty snow that spotted the streets. I just don't know how these poor, miserable, gallant people face their lives. But David is nicer, more considerate, more understanding and warm than I have ever known him. He has become very much like his enchanting father.

February 27 (Written by the light of five candles. Electricity on only after dark.)

Lunched with David. Restrained myself from exploding about the telephone conversation I had with his mother-in-law. Really Vanessa is too maddening. I wanted so much to see Clive [Bell]. He is such fun, makes one feel so attractive. This time I wanted to talk to him about Proust. When he knew I was coming to London he asked me to dine and sent me his country telephone number. I called and an icy feminine voice answered saying that he was in London. So I asked whether this was Vanessa and she said yes. I explained who I was and she said, "I thought Clive had an engagement with you." I said, "Well, I had hoped to see him but I haven't heard from him. Where could I reach him?" She said she had absolutely no idea of where he would be in London. I said he had given me an address in Charlotte Street but that I had lost it. She said, "Oh, yes, he did used to stay with a friend there but *she* has gone away and I don't think he stays there any more. I am very sorry not to be able to help you." Disappointing. She didn't sound the least bit sorry. Granted that it's twenty-five years since we met, I did used to see her nearly every day during the weeks when Duncan [Grant] was painting my portrait in the studio they shared. I always thought she had ice-water in her veins. But that may have been because she condescended to treat me like a rich American who had commissioned a portrait whereas actually it was Duncan who asked to paint me.

Vanessa's rudeness did not leave me in the best humor to greet Harold [Nicolson] who has just left. After considerable hemming and hawing on the telephone he said he would make time to come and see me around seven but that he had to meet someone coming in on the Golden Arrow which arrives around eight. When I remember all the times he came and stayed in Ashfield I do think that as he knew six weeks ago when I was coming, he might have managed to give me a little better welcome. But he was so funny I am still laughing.

He arrived looking very M.P. — Anthony Eden style hat, splendid frogged great-coat with Persian lamb collar. He wore a beautifully tailored, double-breasted, blue serge suit and a blue shirt which fortunately had very long tails. For his fly was wide open. The shirt-tails, however, preserved his modesty.

The real reason I wanted to see Harold was to get a letter of introduction to Proust's friend Antoine Bibesco, who is a friend of Harold's. There was no need for a letter, he said. I could just telephone him. An American woman staying at the Ritz would interest him enough. He is malicious, mean about money, unconventional and a "womanizer" which Harold certainly isn't. He concluded by saying that the Prince Bibesco was quite different from Proust's other aristocratic French friends. With them, he warned me, my spontaneous although charming American manners would not do. I should have to be very correct and careful of how I acted and what I said. At this point he rose to leave and discovered the expanse of blue shirt where his fly should have been.

"Why didn't you tell me?"

"Because I didn't know the correct way to do it."

He had the good grace to burst into laughter. "Vita will be so amused," he said. "She says I've never learned to button up." After consuming considerable Bourbon he departed saying Vita would stop by to see me tomorrow.

Afterthought, 1977

As I re-read this part of my 1947 diary, I wondered why Harold had been so reluctant to call on me. So I looked again at his diary which I had not read since its publication nine years ago. It turns out that that day was a turning point in his life. He had just decided to become a member of the Labour Party. Knowing that his mother, his wife, and his sons would disapprove, he postponed telling them of this step for several days. I now see he could hardly have been expected to explain the situation to an outsider. If he had, I should have regarded his visit as a courtesy rather than as a manifestation of ingratitude.

February 28   Vita [Sackville-West] stopped by in the morning. She was as vague and charming as ever and looked quite beautiful. I gave her the silk stockings, olive oil and soap she asked me to bring and which she took along with her to the centenary services for Ellen Terry. I was surprised at her going to such a public ceremony. I always think of her as a very private person. She invited me to come to Sissinghurst when I come back.

Lunched with David. When I told him I was taking tea today with Mrs. Sydney Schiff he went off into an uncharacteristic diatribe against her late husband. He was a rich Austrian, David said, who had acquired the manners of an old-fashioned English Colonel on stage. At some party David heard him complaining to Wyndham Lewis about the unfairness of the income tax which had reduced him to being a very poor man. "It was the kind of subject," David said, "which Schiff liked talking about to impoverished artists."

Afterthought, 1977

It seems unfair to Sydney Schiff's memory to give only David Garnett's obviously prejudiced picture of him. Apart from being wealthy he was a patron of the arts as well as an editor and writer. Of the four novels he wrote between 1919 and 1924 under the pseudonym Stephen Hudson, two were dedicated to Proust, the first, *Richard Kurt,* before he had met him. Schiff was also editor of the review *Arts and Letters,* and it is evident from Proust's letters to both husband and wife that, although his affection for Violet Schiff was personal, his relationship with Schiff was based at least in part on his professional usefulness. Proust also appreciated their influence in making his work known in England, but what he would have thought of the atrocious translation of *Le temps retrouvé* perpetrated by Mr. Schiff is better left to the imagination. (Fortunately Andreas Mayor's superb rendering of the final volume of the novel has superseded earlier efforts.)

Had Schiff's literary interests been restricted to his own writing and to his helpful friendships with authors he might have left a more attractive image. But like so many rich amateurs of the arts, he craved association with the famous. This taste so often unfortunately manifests itself as a kind of naive snobbery as well as a lack of understanding of artists' relations to one another. Various accounts of the huge supper party given by the Schiffs after the première of Stravinsky's *Renard* to honor Diaghilev and his company, along with the other men of genius the Schiffs most admired —Picasso, Stravinsky, Proust, and Joyce — make lively reading. Proust's questions irritated Stravinsky, who answered rudely. Joyce and Proust in a far from felicitous encounter admitted never having read each other's works. The soirée was, no doubt, a social triumph, but such an agglomeration of genius would seem to be more indicative of the collector's instinct than a love of the arts.

February 28 *(continued)*   I liked Mrs. Schiff. She seems sweet and courageous — badly hurt when her house in the country was bombed. She made me feel nice and warm inside, a feeling I particularly appreciate in London right now. When I told her that I loved Henry James as much as Proust she said she had always wanted to meet the kind of American James wrote about and now her wish had been gratified. I don't suppose that I am like Henrietta Stackpole or Charlotte, and I can't imagine anyone seeing me as Millie or Maggie so it is nice to think that my girlhood fantasy of being like Isabel Archer shone through. Being flattered is so pleasant. Naturally I thought she was very nice, although the unctuousness of Proust's letters to the Schiffs always made me suspect his sincerity about them. In any case, as my brother Lincoln often comments when we disagree about someone, "Nice is nice to me."

March 1   Although it was bitter cold outdoors and I knew the Royal Academy would be unheated, I couldn't bear the idea of leaving London without seeing the King's pictures. I was bound to see the Van Dycks and the Vermeers if it was the last thing I did, and it damn near was. The cold emanating from those icy stone floors is unimaginable. But I was so absorbed in the paintings that I barely noticed it and all of a sudden I had a chill, started sneezing like mad and had to leave.

Afterthought, 1977

This chill, the first of so many to follow, must have been disabling enough to prevent my keeping my diary for five days. So I remember nothing about what must have been a very disturbing, insecure departure for Paris, for me then a friendless city which I had last visited only briefly more than twenty years earlier.

PART
TWO

Chapter 3

March 6 I HAVE NOW been in Paris four days — two of them spent in bed. The surprisingly overheated train between Calais and Paris made my cold so much worse that I could barely breathe or speak when I arrived at the Ritz. I had chosen to stay at this hotel because in his later years Proust frequented it. I didn't really think his ghost would hover, but I did hope to find some trace of his presence, perhaps a concierge who had risen from lift boy or an aged chasseur who would remember Olivier, the legendary maître d'hôtel who supplied Proust with gossip invaluable for his work and to whom he gave an inscribed set of *La recherche*. But my Proustian antennae were dormant. All I could do was fall into bed. Outside it rains and rains. The rooms are very nice — double bedroom with Edwardian brass beds and a small salon with a wood-burning fireplace, green brocade curtains and reproduction Louis XV or XVI furniture all in slippery satin or brocade — no working-size desk, no sofa, no reading light, but the bed is warm and comfortable. Eleven dollars a day at the present exchange for all this luxury is unbelievable.

The servants are very friendly but my French lessons in Boston, intended to prepare me to carry on highbrow conversation, have not made communication with waiters, maids and shopkeepers easy. However, I am improving as I have had all my meals in my room for the first two days — always the same two morning and evening waiters. The food here is a great deal poorer and less plentiful than at the Berkeley or the Ivy or the Etoile in London.

I miss London. I had a new feeling about it this time, as though in some indefinable way it were a small piece of home to me — different from the romantically exciting place David made it seem all those years ago, the healing escape from pre- and post-marital Northampton gossip that Harry and I found in the De Vere Gardens cottage, and totally unlike the disillusioning, indifferent place it seemed in 1936. Now I feel as though it were an intrinsic, very deep part of my whole being.

These thoughts came to me after one of the waiters responded to my question about the time for the radio news. "They don't give us any news," he said. "It's not the workers' fault that there aren't any newspapers. It's the fault of the government. They don't want us to know what they're doing." In England there's plenty of carping against the government, but not on the level of fooling the people, merely for inefficiency and bungling.

March 8   Mme. Bradley came to tea today. I was very frightened of meeting her. She is the only person to whom I had a letter of introduction here and that was on a purely business level as she is to be my literary agent. What scared me was a brotherly remark of Lincoln's saying he didn't think we'd get along because she was much too *grande dame* for me. Well, she is a *grande dame*. I'd like to be one just like her. She is the widow of the American writer and translator William Aspenwall Bradley, who became the literary agent of Joyce, Hemingway, Gertrude Stein and dozens of other well-known authors. Jenny Bradley, who is French, took over the business when he died. She either knows everybody I want to meet or somebody who does. I found her warm and kind and cordial. I think she is amused at my nonacademic approach to acquiring material for footnotes. She is arranging for me to meet as many people as possible right away.

2

March 10　　A day or two after Mme. Bradley was here I had a telephone call from the Princesse Marthe Bibesco who lives in the hotel and who wrote a flowery little book about Proust some twenty years ago. She said would I come up to her little hovel to talk to her at 5:30 on Monday. Her little hovel being on the floor above mine, it didn't occur to me to have myself announced, and at about 5:40, dressed in my Mainbocher frock, a rather elegant little hat and Ma's sables, I had myself lifted up to the next floor so as to benefit in social prestige in the eyes of the lift boy, having to ask him which was *appartement cent cinquante*. It turned out to be what was formerly a servant's room from the days when people traveled with personal maids and valets.

I knocked on the door, was told to come in, and there on the chaise longue among dozens of pots of hyacinths and great vases of branches behind her head lay the Princesse, an ample, handsome, distinguished-looking woman, about sixty. Her head was swathed, à la Queen Marie of Rumania, in a white lace scarf caught nun-like at the chin. She wore a rather elegant garment, half Chinese mandarin, half monk's robe. In a *fauteuil* at her feet sat a very fat and quite soiled priest. She looked at me in astonishment so I explained who I was and that I thought that this was the day she had asked me to come. She said that she thought I would have myself announced and that I wasn't coming until 5:30. I said that it was just my American bad manners that had made me fail to be announced, that it was quarter to six but that I would be glad to come another day. No indeed, said she, she longed to talk to me about Marcel Proust and as long as I was in the hotel would I mind if she called me in about twenty minutes.

At the end of an hour and a half she called me. I again offered to come another day but she insisted that I come in ten minutes. There was a man there, but he didn't matter. She would send him away, she said. Fortunately for him he doesn't understand English. He turned out to be a moving-picture man, very attractive and charming, who had come to talk to her about making her biography of Maximilian and Carlotta into a film. This was a shock to me because I thought only Hollywood people were stupid enough to pay out good money for books about subjects in the public domain.

Her hovel turned out really to be one — a small bed-sitter with a maid running around in it, not conducive to the smooth flow of conversation. The moving-picture man left after she explained at length how busy she was — her publisher coming tomorrow morning to sign the contract for her next book and in the afternoon she must go to see her old and dear friend Paul Claudel inducted into the Academy which had finally persuaded him to accept membership much against his will. Then she turned her attention to me and said I could see what a hovel she had, that I, no doubt, had a large suite on the first floor. I said no, I merely had a bedroom and a room in which to work on the fourth floor. I also said that when she went to England I hoped that she would not tell our friend Harold Nicolson that I had had the bad manners to come up to her room unannounced as he had warned me about my informal American manners.

"Not at all," said she, "it was I who was rude." "Ain't it the truth, sister?" thought I, and said nothing. She then went on to explain that the priest was here from Rumania, that she, too, was a Catholic, that he was bringing her news of her people there and that since I could see there was only one *fauteuil* it was clear that she couldn't ask him to get up and give it to me. The straight chair into which she had put the moving-picture man obviously doesn't count. Then she asked me about my book. She said that she was about to publish a little essay on Proust, the manuscript of which she at that point picked up and handed me, after removing it from a very amateurishly crayoned paper cover. It was based, she said, on the letters of her cousin the Duc de Guiche who was a great friend of Proust's and in them lay the real key to the Duchesse de Guermantes and also the link between Proust and Chateaubriand. I wanted to ask her to let me take those few typewritten sheets — it will be the slenderest of volumes — to read tonight and to return in the morning. But I was just as Rumanian as she was. I asked when it was to be published, and when she said in a magazine in June and in book form during the summer I said I would certainly have to arrange to get a copy. She then said that if I would translate it and see to its publication in America she would give it to me right away. I told her that I never had anything to do with business matters, that Mme. Bradley looked after all that sort of thing. "Oh, I know Mme. Bradley," she said. "It was she who asked me to see you, wasn't it?"

We talked a little more about Proust — conversation consisting largely of quotations by her from letters which I also know by heart since I had spent days on end translating them. When I left she took me to the door, made me promise I would find out from the concierge when she returned from England at the end of April so that I could call her and make another appointment. I said that I would be very shy about calling her, that she could see from my not having had myself announced that I was really very gauche about that sort of thing. Whereupon I must admit she did crash through like a lady and say that I had been very gracious

and kind to come up after she had sent me away
but that socially she was so "unsophisticated." I
could have wept with pleasure at that word. She is
what my mother in a German phrase would have
called *"in alle Wasser gewaschen."* As I left to
walk downstairs the Princesse said my hat made me
look like Ceres, which shows, I suppose, that the
old earth-mother quality shines right through my
efforts at style, if shines is the word.

Afterthought, 1977

It occurs to me as I re-read this passage in my diary that a
present-day reader is unlikely to have any frame of reference for
the Princesse Marthe Bibesco, a fact that she would have found
unbelievable. Permanently endowed with the assurance of her
beauty as recorded in her youth by the painter Boldini, a portrait
reproduced in many books, she luxuriated in utter self-confidence. Intelligent — Proust said that intelligence for her was
another form of *coquetterie* — a facile writer, with an uninhibited talent for combining fact and fiction, her redoubtable charm
insured her fame if not in the end her fortune. Among her
lovers were said to have been the Crown Prince of Germany
and Ramsay MacDonald. But such rumors can never be veri-
fied. They merely serve to show the caliber of her reputation,
which was based on her literary as well as her personal glamour.

The substance of her book *Au bal avec Marcel Proust* made
meeting her seem desirable, although now that I re-read it for
the first time in forty years I must admit that I was sufficiently
charmed then by the fairy-tale element to ignore how few pages
of her own composition filled out the body of the book. Actually,
although it includes Proust's few inordinately flattering letters
to her which at the time I lacked the background to evaluate, the
importance of the contents lay in the inclusion of Marcel's letters
to his very close friends, the Princesse' cousins, Antoine and Em-

manuel Bibesco. Previously unpublished, they were obviously of first-rate importance in any collection of his letters although undated and incomplete. My eventual gaining access to the original letters involved adventure and intrigue that will be recounted farther on in this book.

Intrigue as a technique was an essential part of Marthe's nature, and it was the quality which finally turned me against her. A few years after our first meeting, the Princesse and I were again neighbors in the same building. But by that time any relationship existing between us was to her advantage rather than mine. The calculated insistence with which she persisted in trying to lure me into her apartment to cross-question me about my friendship with her recently deceased cousin, Antoine, changed my original amused detachment into active dislike.

Since I am therefore unable to give the reader a fair picture of this distinguished adventuress I shall compensate by quoting from her obituary, which appeared in the *Figaro* on November 30, 1973:

> The Princess Marthe Bibesco died Wed. evening at her Paris residence. Born in Bucharest in 1888, she was the daughter of Jean Lahovary, Rumanian minister to France. After being educated by a French governess she married the Prince Bibesco, son of the reigning prince of Walachia. After her marriage, she came to live in the Ile Saint-Louis where she received in her salon the greatest writers of the 20th century whose silhouettes she drew in elegant and lively books. She acquired celebrity in 1924 with the publication of *Le Perroquet vert*. This was followed by such autobiographical novels as *Catherine Paris* (1927) and *Feuilles de calendrier* (1939) in which she described the cosmopolitan aristocracy she met in Paris ... Her novel *Katia* was made into a film in 1938 by Maurice Tourneur, the heroine of which was

played by Danielle Darrieux ... The Princess also left some engaging essays on Marcel Proust and Paul Claudel. Member of the Royal Academy of Belgium and of the *Société des gens de Lettres,* the Princess was the recipient of many literary honors. She was also a Knight of the Legion of Honor and commander of *la Couronne de Belgique.*

Lest this formal obituary seem tinged by my own coolness I quote from a column by Michel Robida entitled "An Egeria of Europe: Marthe Bibesco" which appeared in the *Figaro* on the first anniversary of her death.

> Some times a child is suddenly confronted with a being who embodies the qualities he prefers above all others. This encounter remains with him his whole life through. Thus there appeared before me one day a dazzling young woman. I saw her enter my mother's salon, superb, glowing in silver scarves. She was called the Princesse Bibesco and she was radiant with the rarely combined gifts of beauty, elegance, wealth and wit ...
>
> From the delta of the Danube and the Palace of Mogosëa ... her trajectory led her, after flashing her way across Europe and other parts of the planet, to the shores of the Loire, after a stop on the banks of the Seine. For the last year the Princesse Bibesco has lain in the Ménars cemetery, and I have not ceased remembering a question she asked: "Do you think that confined in my tomb I shall no longer be able to remember the perfume of a hyacinth?"

That question about the hyacinths reminds me of an attribute of the Princesse' that did charm me. Her love of flowers expressed itself in a delightfully original fashion. Instead of bouquets or large arrangements she placed on her mantelpiece and on tables dozens of small vases, each just large enough to hold a single flower. And after reading M. Robida's article I am reminded that one day when my resistance was low and I accepted one of her frequent invitations to come up to her apartment above mine in the Quai de Bourbon, each vase held a hyacinth. They perfumed the room. The aesthetic appeal of their pastel colors and their aroma somehow eased the impact of her brash questioning and enabled me to practice an uncharacteristic conversational evasiveness.

3

March 11   Today I lunched in the kind of house that Proust must have frequented in his youth. Now it is the British Officers' Club, next to the Embassy. It used to belong to one of the Rothschilds and makes Lansdowne House look like a cottage. Even the Frick Museum is simple compared to it, although the murals there are rather superior.

I went with Stuart Gilbert who at first seems very dried up and over-British, but after a cocktail and wine opens up and is most interesting. For twenty years he was a judge in India. Then he came here, fell in love with Paris as only an Englishman can and married a French wife. He helped translate *Ulysses* into French and was a great friend of Joyce. He has a movie scenario of *Ulysses* that he and Joyce did together. It sounds marvelous as he told me about it.

At six I went to call on the Duchesse de Clermont-Tonnerre in her shabby but elegant apartment in the rue de la Faisanderie. The small drawing room was unheated and no lights were turned on. When she first came in, wearing a very smart black suit, she didn't seem over fifty — slender, her short hair dyed mustard color. Actually she must be nearly eighty and after a few minutes you realize how old and bent, almost blind and rather deaf she is. Her voice and speech, both French and English, are very beautiful. For facts about Proust's life outside of her own experience she is limited, but her own personal information, her stories and her wit are delightful. I can't, of course, take notes in this social kind of research, which doesn't matter too much as she said very little about Proust that hasn't long since been published in her books. But her stories about M. and Mme. Straus are unforgettable. When someone asked Mme. Straus why among all her suitors she chose Straus, she replied, *"Pour me débarrasser de lui."* He knew that she never loved him and that she had a number of love affairs. But he always said that when she was old she would belong to him alone. After her death Mme. de C-T said that she took two handkerchiefs to dry his tears when she went to comfort him. *"Quand même, c'est mieux comme ceci,"* he said. *"Elle avait commencé à me coûter très cher."* The Duchesse's comment: *"Il n'est plus qu'un vieil avare."* Balzac would have liked that even better than Proust, I think.

I asked her whether Proust hadn't merely added an "n" to Swan, the name of the drug manufacturer whose family still have the same retail store in the rue de Castiglione that was there in Proust's youth. She didn't know these people, she said, and added that Proust wasn't at all a snob. He was simply born into one circle and fell in love with another. It was like two clubs, she said, each equally good in its own way, but no one then belonged to both. He was the great exception and that was why so many people envied and hated him.

I told her about the Proust group in the Amherst College faculty which meets regularly to read aloud portions of the *Recherche,* each person playing the part of one of the characters. This juxtaposition of Proust and Emily Dickinson whom she also greatly admires amused her enough to say that she would like to come to lunch with me next week.

She poured me out a little thimble glass of wine and offered some big, thick soda biscuits which I refused, knowing how hard they are to get. There were no apologies or explanations. It was really in the grand manner. As I left in the dark after seven she turned on the lights.

Afterthought, 1977

Putting myself back into the frame of mind in which I went to see Mme. de Clermont-Tonnerre I am struck by the limiting, not to say obsessive, attitude that research engenders. From what I wrote thirty years ago no one would guess that she was one of the most distinguished *grandes dames* of France, as well as a talented writer. Of course I knew this, having read her memoirs — *Au temps des équipages* and *Les marronniers en fleurs* — as well as her book that was my text, *Robert de Montesquiou et Marcel Proust.*

Daughter of the Duc de Gramont, descended from one of the oldest, most aristocratic families in France, stepdaughter of a Rothschild, Elisabeth Gramont's birthright gave her entry into the highest circles of society, not only in France but in England

and on the continent as well. Her awareness of her inheritance freed her of any false pride or snobbery. Indeed, one of the charms of her memoirs is an absence of any conceit or unconscious arrogance that approaches humility. Here is her description of her introduction to the literary worlds in which she became friends with writers as different as Marcel Proust, Paul Valéry, and Natalie Barney.

> It was at Mme. de Caillavet's in the circle where Anatole France lived and thought, that I first became aware of the astonishing diversity of the compartments into which most French people shut themselves. The rather scandalized surprise my presence and M. de Clermont-Tonnerre's evoked in the salon of the avenue Hoche stupefied me. What secret, terrible reasons were there to make a young couple swap polo and the races for the Caillavet Sundays? . . . For me the idea of seeing, of listening to the author of *Le Lys rouge, L'Etui de nacre, La Rôtisserie de la Reine Pédauque,* was not natural . . . I thought of Anatole France as an abstraction, as remote as Buddha, Plato, or Renan. He was a mythical figure everyone talked about, whose books everyone read but who unlike everybody else couldn't sit down in an armchair, lunch with his neighbors, receive money from his publishers, buy a hat or yawn behind a newspaper.

Although it was easy for a foreigner to be introduced to the great man, Mme. de Clermont-Tonnerre wrote, it was difficult for a native French person, who might turn into an encumbrance. Her recently published translation of Keats' poems gave Elisabeth Gramont entrée to the circle which led to her welcome in other literary salons.

She first met Proust as a very young man in the salon of Mme. Straus, who was the mother of Marcel's schoolmate Jacques Bizet, son of her first husband, Georges Bizet. But their friendship began several years later and endured throughout his life. She wrote about him appreciatively, with subtle perception and without the self-involvement or bias of some of his friends and critics. Here is an example of her discernment and style:

Proust delighted in the study of servants. Was it because they supplied him with unsuspected grist for his mill? Or did he envy their opportunity for a closer knowledge of the objects of his studies? In any case, domestics, their personalities and their looks afforded him an amusing puppet-show . . . He is the first, perhaps the only writer since Molière who has treated this special class superlatively in depth . . .

At his request, I wrote Proust about how as a child I was dazzled by the luxurious staff of a country neighbor: "His footmen dressed from early morning in blue panne velvet knee-breeches, their blond hair iron-curled: they inspired us with such overwhelming admiration that we never dared ask any such service of them as launching boats, holding horses for us to mount, or fetching a hat from the garden. We respected the ineffectual beauty of these blue statues."

To this description Proust replied, "Your letter is a true Watteau, a true *Fête Galante* by Verlaine (who was particularly susceptible to footmen in blue panne velvet). I should return it to you and will hold it at your disposal, for you should publish it, if not separately at least enshrined in one of your books . . ."

He returned my letter and his reply reveals the tendency to that compulsive empathy of which he gave a thousand examples to others . . . He needed this sentimental hypertrophy for his work. Transposed into everyday life it gave place to those demonstrations of affection, of admiration, and politeness of which he was so prodigal. He managed even to get into improbable states of rage or compassion. With the same rapture he would thank a lady for some little expression that pleased him and express in these terms his gratitude to a cultivated stranger who had supplied him with information about Henry James: "And always, the image I keep seeing again is you, you who are probably the being I love the most in the world . . ."!!! But underneath all that I think he had a large store of indifference: people were for him too exciting objects of study to permit his becoming attached to them. "There are no longer anything but eccentric types who amuse and instruct me," he wrote me.

In *Robert de Montesquiou et Marcel Proust* Mme. de Clermont-Tonnerre described Proust from a personal point of view as a man and a friend. Appraising him as an artist in her second volume of memoirs, she gives a brief and brilliant description of his great novel, which should entice even reluctant readers to venture beyond *Swann's Way*.

There is only one way to understand and love Marcel Proust; to read and re-read him, go over his prefaces, remind oneself of what he has said: one will perceive a thousand things one never felt before reading him. Of his own work he said "As a book, it really bears no resemblance to the classic novel . . ." It is not a story you hurry through to discover the unwinding of the plot. It is a miraculous promenade reaching from the earth to the heavens and descending to the depths of the sea. A reader who opens one one of the ten volumes of *A la recherche du temps perdu* will find himself in immediate contact with live human flux.

High society, good people, vicious horrors, beaches, the countryside, Paris restaurants, the Dreyfus Affair, musical sensations and incomparable descriptions of paintings; human clockwork, accurate physiology; the unknown, mystery, déjà vu freshly viewed through extraordinary eyes; morning in the *Bois,* servants, some chauffeurs, doctors, *grands bourgeois,* an old woman lavatory attendant, a great diplomat, Sarah Bernhardt, writers, outdated *salons,* a delightful little girl, young girls who frolic like boys, provincials who peep out their curtains to see what's happening in the street, family life; love, jealousy that stretches out like an octopus in the middle of the book; longing for voyages more than the actual voyages, atlases and automobiles, a telephone conversation like no other — all this he brought into his sick-room . . .

But far from literary thoughts filled my mind as I left Mme. de Clermont-Tonnerre's that evening.

4

March 14   I have been here twelve days now and have dined alone in my salon every night. Gradually I have got over the panic induced, I suppose, by being ill in bed at the start. Then there is the daily rigamarole about permission to work in the Bibliothèque Nationale and the indifferent food every night. I have discovered the solution to the latter problem. You must not order the regular meal — only the extras which are no more expensive if the price is listed. If there is no price they are bound to cost too much. But the calves' liver, the kidneys, the cold ham, the bacon and eggs, and quite a number of egg dishes are always very nice and the endive salad is plentiful. But there is no fruit at all and the meat is apt to be vile. But tonight I did have an excellent minuscule tournedos.

I do need a decent meal at night on the days when I lunch on bread and cheese and some wine which I take with me to the library, following the example of the people around me. Even saving time by not going out to lunch one can only work two or three hours a day. There is no heat, no electric light, no daylight except from the windows in the dome which haven't been cleaned since before the war. So reading the print of Proust's articles in old, yellow newspapers is hell on the eyes. And the red tape to get them takes so much time. There are four or five catalogues each with a different method. However, the secretary whom Bob Linscott [publisher's editor] recommended has appeared and is helpful, although she knows a good deal less French than he said. After three days of struggle she appears to have mastered the use of the many different colored request slips which vary according to what day and what time you want a book. But in spite of all the physical discomfort and complications it is exciting to read the articles that until now have just been referred to in the letters.

The newspaper room smells strange because it harbors so many derelicts sleeping or drinking wine behind their papers. The *gardiens* are all war veterans, little Hitlers, who bully the derelicts and, unless tipped, forget to bring the volumes one has ordered. I think wistfully sometimes of Widener, Houghton and the Athenaeum. But the working conditions don't really bother me. What I loathe is the prohibition atmosphere.

I was forewarned never to cash checks at a bank

and have already used my letter of introduction to an "honest" black market bootlegger. Such a fine, reliable fellow with a shop that can't sell anything because prices are too high for Americans to buy. But I hate this business of deciding how much money to change today because you might get more francs tomorrow. David complained that in London there wasn't even an efficient black market. You can't buy a single thing there without coupons except jewelry and books. Here everything is rationed, too, but nobody ever asks for a coupon. One of the waiters said to me that if only they could get rid of the black market he wouldn't care how stiff the rationing was. But in both cases it is equally untrue. It would be quite against David's nature to use the black market, and the French could never be made to discipline themselves as the English do. That is why, although London for a city that was once so beautiful is now the most tragic, somber, grim, ugly city one can imagine, it isn't frightening the way Paris is because it is an expression of the lives and feelings of the people. Here in this architectural marvel of beauty, shabby, unpainted, and tired as it looks, with its appearance of calm and order, the people are fear ridden, insecure and desperate. How do I know this? Partly through my pores and partly through conversations with servants in the hotel, with shop assistants, shop proprietors, taxi drivers, rare as they are. And these are all people who come in contact with what few foreigners there are around. A girl in a shop where I am having a dressing gown made said to me today, *"En Amerique on est heureux, n'est-ce pas? Ici on ne rit plus. Je pense qu'il n'y a plus personne en*

France qui ne voudrait pas aller aux Etats-Unis."

There have been no newspapers for a month in Paris except American and English, and last Monday, when the *Trib* and *The Daily Mail* don't publish, there wasn't a newspaper in Paris because the fog prevented the London papers from being brought over. That with the Moscow conference going on. And the radio news is very poor — way over the heads of most of the people who don't own radios anyway.

Chapter 4

March 15   TODAY I MET Mme. Scheikévitch, who telephoned me at Mme. Bradley's instigation. I had read Mme. S.'s memoirs which depict her not only as a beauty but as that rare being, a *femme du monde* who both reads and writes. Her Paris salon was peopled by a wide range of writers and artists — from Anatole France and d'Annunzio to Paul Valéry and Jean Cocteau. Mme. Bradley warned me that she had never been as attractive as she thought she was and had spent all her money on the luxuries of her salon. But in spite of being hard up, run down at the heels, hypochrondriacal and inclined to complain, she retains her intelligence, her gifts as both listener and talker. She knew I would find her very helpful. And indeed I do. Just the things she told me about Proust today show how he collected information for his work, how utilitarian his social life really was.

He was like an entomologist on the hunt, she said. At first she would be flattered by his elaborate, formalized compliments. But gradually she would become aware of the transition from polite questions to an almost scientific interrogation. Sometimes he would ask her to interpret some passage in Dostoevski. Then suddenly catching her unawares he would become embarrassingly personal. "Are you eating quite well today, my dear? . . . Are you eating properly? That little pimple on your cheek? — Really your skin is too beautiful to be marred like that. Is your food too acid? Is your digestion good? Are you regular, etc.?" he would ask. And then just as she would be recovering from this extraordinary clinical invasion of privacy, he would already have shifted the level of conversation on to another plane even more personal. About jealousy, say.

Mme. S. was married young to Pierre Carolus-Duran, son of the successful portrait painter. But her marriage was brief because of her husband's infidelity. The details of her attempted suicide were Paris gossip for some time and Proust well knew that the subject of jealousy would be painful to her. But he was writing *La prisonnière* and *Albertine disparue* and must have regarded himself as fortunate to be able to acquire such first-hand information.

If a beautiful young woman's husband deserted her for another woman, if her anguish was so great that she was driven to attempt suicide, if she still bore the scar on her breast where the bullet had luckily failed to penetrate, how had she felt? Was it this or that way or still a third? Mme. S. said she felt like an insect still vibrating under a microscope. There was no escape from the relentless questioning. Almost as if hypnotized, she would reveal herself under the X-ray of his mind until the pain became intolerable. Then she would involuntarily burst into tears. "Yes, that is the way I thought it would be," he would say. "That is how I imagined it." Then shocked and embarrassed by her weeping, he would abandon his role as inquisitor. Once more he would become the soothing, sympathetic friend, *homme du monde,* smothering her with his characteristically exaggerated flattery.

Only one person, Mme. S. said, Céleste Albaret, his *gouvernante* for the last ten years of his life, could give an idea of Proust's speech. She is a marvelous mimic and unconsciously acquired the rhythm of his words, his sentences, his speech. Mme. S. is going to take me to meet her soon.

Afterthought, 1977

The irony of Céleste's being the first person to whom Mme. Scheikévitch introduced me did not occur to me at the time. For then I was preoccupied with what she could tell me about Proust and didn't try to visualize her as the prestigious *salonnière* she had once been. But today, as I happened by chance to be reading Paul Morand's *Journal d'un Attaché d'Ambassade* I have found a number of entries that bring to life the difference between the nostalgic aging woman I knew and the glamorous *femme du monde* she had been.

Her guests whom Proust's friend, the literary diplomat Paul Morand, recorded after the many lunch parties and dinners he attended at her home represented many different groups: the politicians Aristide Briand and Philippe Berthelot, permanent Secretary of Foreign Affairs; many writers, among them Edith Wharton, Henry Bernstein; the painter Boutet de Monvel, and a number of such social lights as the Duchesse de Lévis-Mirepoix, the Princesse Lucien Murat, Boni de Castellane, the Marquis de Flers, the Princesse Soutzo, and the Abbé Mugnier, who graced all circles.

The entry in Morand's journal for November 11, 1916, explains the charm her Russian origin exercised: "Marie Scheiké-vitch at thirty-five is still very little girl, letting her long hair down on the slightest provocation . . . She talked about having known Tolstoi. She remembers his meeting with her father one cold winter day in Moscow. Tolstoi said, 'Tchaikovsky is dead.' And two great tears (for everything about him is larger than nature, she said) rolled down his cheeks. The little girl wondered whether the tears would freeze when they reached the bottom of his cheeks."

March 15
(continued) I must write down something Mme. de C-T told me that I forgot. At an afternoon musicale Proust came in like a convalescent resuming life, sat next to her and said, "I don't know anybody here. Who is that mousey lady?" — "That's Mme. X." — "And that one there, who's she?" — "Mme. de Brantes." He was startled for a moment, the Duchesse said. Then he exclaimed, "Of course, Mme. de Brantes! I knew her well. The Mme. de Brantes who took all the credit for the Council of Trent is dead, but she is succeeded by this beautiful, tall young woman, who now frequents the salons under the same name as the other and when spoken to probably says, 'Yes, my poor mother-in-law . . .'" When Mme. de C-T read *Le temps retrouvé* she felt sure that that musicale had been seminal for the book.

2

March 18 Life is full of splendid contrasts. After dining alone the whole of the two weeks I've been here, last night I went to a most elegant dinner party. Julian and Juliet Huxley very kindly invited me sight

unseen merely on the strength of a letter of introduction from May Sarton and a telephone conversation. It was an official dinner at the Maison
de l'UNESCO, the most distinguished gathering
I have ever been part of and the Huxleys couldn't
be nicer people. The British Ambassador and Lady
Diana Duff-Cooper were there. She looked just
like the professional beauty she is, still working
hard at it and not unsuccessfully. There were a
number of distinguished French judges, a priest,
André Siegfried, the Countess Palffy, a very beautiful young woman dressed in a long hunter's-green
velvet dress cut like a nineteenth-century side-
saddle riding habit. I was the only American and
sat two seats away from Huxley between a young
Norwegian sociologist and a M. Joxe who was the
perfect person for me. He is a most attractive man
who also happens to be the son-in-law of Daniel
Halévy who went to school with Proust, who owns
the Mme. Straus letters and whom I was just about
to try and arrange to see. So he is going to arrange
everything for me and also is going to give me a
letter to the head of the Bibliothèque Nationale
who will tell me about any manuscripts, etc., that
they may have. M. Joxe assured me he spoke no
English so I spoke my labored French more than
halfway through dinner — wonderful food and
wines. Then when I couldn't find a certain word
he promptly supplied it in English. It turns out that
he has lectured at Harvard and knows English well.
I gather that before he offered to do anything for
me he wanted to test my capacities. He assures me
that my theories about Mme. Straus are all absolutely true. And he said I could discuss everything
with M. Halévy, which is marvelous for me.

After dinner I was introduced to an impressive, obviously very wealthy Frenchman called Henry Gouïn who has a thirteenth-century monastery which he is giving over as a sort of international cultural hostel that will have scholarships. He asked me for American names and I must write Lincoln about it. He will know just the right people to send.

Today I was supposed to meet Monroe [Wheeler] at six but at five-thirty I was seeing a publisher over near the Place St.-Michel. As I was wandering around looking for a taxi I noticed a terrible fire-trap of a theatre with a poster of Marlene Dietrich in front. The film was called *Femme ou Diable*. It turned out to be my favorite picture in the world, *Destry Rides Again,* which, of course, I couldn't resist. No one should miss cowboy French. I had a wonderful time, and only when I came out at eight did I remember about Monroe. But he was having tea here with someone anyway so it didn't matter.

March 19   Before I left home I said to somebody that the kind of lady who goes from one Ritz hotel to another was not at all the kind of me I thought I'd ever turn into. And indeed my choosing to stay here was essentially part of my Proust research. Until today — having never gone any further than the lobby on the Place Vendôme side — I wondered what had made the Ritz name a symbol for elegance and chic. The atmosphere seemed dowdy, well bred and comfortable. But today for the first time I discovered the back entrance on the rue Cambon. Here is the famous bar I used to read about in the '20s — Hemingway, Fitzgerald *et al.* — not very crowded at five o'clock, and then a long *allée* lined with *vitrines* full of all kinds of articles of luxury. This led into a huge hall filled with tea tables and the loud chatter of many dozen made-up, got-up French and international *schweinerei*. I am glad I didn't discover it before I became attached to the friendly routine upstairs and Robert, the paternal concierge on the Vendôme side. I am too Proust-directed not to be discomfited by any changes since his death.

One thing that hasn't changed is the attitude of the servants. The waiter comes in and says, "Madame, there is nothing fit for you to eat on the menu," which is quite true. So I have my regular supper of some sort of pale green *potage*, excellent cold ham, and endive salad. He says he doesn't see how I live and I tell him that last night I went to Prunier's where I had frogs legs, grilled salmon and *petit pois paysannes*, a half bottle of ordinary white wine, all of which cost me around seven dollars. He then tells me of a meal of five courses which he gets near his house for 200 francs. But since that is miles away he tells me of a little place near here where he has a friend in the kitchen who says that the cooking is good and tomorrow when he comes to work he will look at the prices and let me know. This kind of friendliness is really why I like living here, apart from the fact that my rooms are sunny and divinely quiet.

3

March 20 Lunch with Mme. Bradley at her beautiful house on the Ile St.-Louis. We seem to have fallen into the kind of instant friendship that Henry Adams described after his first meeting with Clarence King. She is very busy and I don't see her a great deal but she telephones almost every day and is vastly amused by my adventures. She has a kind of all-encompassing warmth and intelligence that I cherish.

My account of what seemed to me a windfall with M. Joxe made Jenny laugh. She said he was a notorious tease, that the last thing in the world he would do would be to help me meet M. Halévy. I knew Joxe was a dedicated Gaullist but I didn't know that his father-in-law had been a Pétainist, at least a luke-warm one. Although M. Halévy used his influence at Vichy to help many Jews, both French and German, to escape, Joxe has not spoken to him in years. I feel as though I'd been a naive idiot, and as M. Halévy is one of the few people Jenny doesn't know, I shall have to make my own arrangements to meet him.

Last night I went to the Vienna Opera production of *Don Giovanni,* the opera I love best in the world. Visually and musically it was splendid although the interpretation and acting were in the flattest convention. But as a whole it was perfection compared to the Met and it makes you ashamed when you think of the condition of Vienna and what these people have been through that with much less money and energy they can do a so much better job than the Met.

It is midnight and I have just returned from a positively hilarious performance of *Hamlet* at the Marigny Theatre. Jean-Louis Barrault conceives the play as melodrama and plays Hamlet as totally hysterical from the time the ghost appears right through to Ophelia's funeral. Homosexuality is emphasized to a degree that makes Ophelia merely a supernumerary character. Rosencrantz and Guildenstern are SS guards; and whereas a great many scenes were played merely in curtained alcoves, for the scene with his mother the whole huge stage was used as a bedroom with the widest bed and the most colossal headboard imaginable. The climax of the scene was not the killing of Polonius but Hamlet jumping up and down on the bed tearing an endless amount of bedding to pieces.

Gide's prose translation precluded any element of poetry. One can only wonder what impression is made on the dozens of G.I.'s who were there, most of whom had probably never read it in English. I can only remember a few of the translation's phrases that sounded ludicrous: *"Fragilité! ton nom est femme!"* *"La reine encarnouflée"* for Hecuba "the mobled queen." "Get thee to a nunnery" reduced to *"Entre au couvent."* But most chilling and inappropriate Horatio's final words, *"Bonne nuit, gentil Prince."* The connotations of the word *gentil* against that stage full of dead bodies was really too much. Early in the play Horatio called Hamlet *"mon doux Seigneur"* and that sounded all right.

4

March 21   Mme. Scheikévitch came for lunch. She's terribly nice, infinitely helpful and equally embarrassing. If only she weren't quite so down at the heel and so articulate about her straitened circumstances I could more easily accept her compliments. God knows, I am susceptible to flattery but I do like it to be based on a slightly longer acquaintance.

She brought me a copy of the first edition of her letters from Proust — very rare and long out of print — inscribed to M.C. whose *"lumineuse intelligence a si bien compris l'oeuvre de M.P., et qui est si digne de la commenter."* How the hell she should think this of me after a single meeting during which she did all the talking I'm sure I don't know.

In the afternoon she took me to meet Comte Robert de Billy at his impressive huge *hôtel particulier.* In the large garden stood a colossal Buddha and many other oriental sculptures. He was a very old friend of Proust's, in the foreign service most of his life, at one time ambassador to Japan. He has collected rare books and all sorts of oriental objects of art. Outside of a museum or the rare-book room of a library, I have never seen, or rather half seen, such beautiful things. He didn't turn on a light until six o'clock and then only one small bulb in his vast library. He is a tall, rather formidable figure, seventy-eight years old, with the liveliest possible mind. He speaks perfect English, as do all the aristocracy I've met so far. He showed me Proust manuscripts and first editions and suggested a point about the illustrations for my book which is interesting and valuable. He said I should try to get a photograph showing Proust's smile even when his health was bad and he was in pain. The smile was slightly mocking and often accompanied a description of some person or an amusing story.

During the last years of his life this expression was rare. It occurred when he had made some humorous discovery that made him laugh occasionally but never unkindly.

There was nothing of the character M. de Norpois about M. de Billy, but I am sure that Proust drew much of his information about the diplomatic service from this friend who served in so many different countries. He amused me by writing in the copy of his book which I took along with me that I knew more about Proust's letters than he did. I have obviously read them more recently as his book, of which they formed the core, came out nearly twenty years ago.

March 22   I am very discouraged about finishing the work I want to do here before I have to leave. Although there have been continual promises that the current will be turned on in the B.N. each day, so far there has been light only when the sun shines, which is intermittently. And the eyestrain from reading the faded print of old newspapers and periodicals is very wearing. Late this afternoon to everyone's astonishment the lights flickered briefly. But the bulbs are so feeble they won't be much help. Besides, the library closes from Good Friday through Easter Monday and then again for the *clôture annuelle* from April 15 to May 1.

The longer I stay here the more the character and temperament of the French puzzle me. Verbally they are the most courteous people in the world but physically the rudest. Nobody thinks anything of knocking you off the pavement, of kicking you black and blue in a theatre aisle or banging a door in your face. They are endlessly

inventive and brilliant and logical but they seem
to have no interest in documentation or history in
anything but the most traditional sense. Not one
newspaper has a morgue. *Paris-Soir* had a very
inadequate one before the war but that's gone.
There is no index to periodical literature or newspapers so that an endless amount of valuable scholarly information is lost unless it happens to be
available in book form. And most of these books
are no longer in print and probably never will be
reprinted. If it weren't for Douglas Alden's Ph.D.
thesis with its exhaustive Proust bibliography
through 1935 I could never have started to cover
the field. But starting in '30 with a few literary
weeklies I have managed to collect some stuff that
seems to have evaded other people.

I had lunch at a restaurant I noticed the other
day behind the Madeleine. Everybody reads all
the menus that are posted outside each restaurant,
even the Ritz, and compares prices and choice of
dishes which vary greatly. I noticed that for the
first time there were radishes — they stopped serving them because they assume that no one would
eat them without butter — and *Bouquet d'écre-
visses,* those wonderful tiny shrimpish crabs that
you eat in your fingers. So I went in. It turned
out to be a large middle- and working-class place
on two floors. Saturday is a wonderful day to lunch
out alone in Paris because almost all the other
lunchers are people in love. Last week at the place
I went they were all middle-aged businessmen with
their *midinette* mistresses barely able to get through
their lunch in their eagerness for bed. Today they
were rather sedate, working-class engaged couples
— a French soldier and his girl, an Indonesian pair,

the girl partly European, caramel color and lovely, and a white collar pair, the girl, dowdy, with the zipper on her skirt undone, so in love with the guy, who loved her too, but not in the same way, that she couldn't keep her hands off him and kept straightening his tie or his pocket handkerchief or looking at his wrist watch. It was very touching. There was also a Norwegian pair being entertained by two very agreeable, bearded Frenchmen. Their common language was English of a variety that nearly caused me to lose an ear it was so funny. There are quite a few English wandering around the deserted streets, having crossed the Channel in a hurricane yesterday to try and get a little warmth and sunshine. Poor creatures, I hope they get it. I don't know how they have ever survived their winter.

Around six I went to a most elegant gathering given by M. Henry Gouïn, whom I had met at the Huxley dinner. But the French seem to assume that you wouldn't be there if you didn't know everybody else. M. Gouïn was cordial but I was left to wander by myself. The house is quite new, modern, glass and marble, the drawing room, largely windows, so large that the twenty or thirty guests looked rather like ants. The occasion, I gathered, had to do with the establishment of M. Gouïn's property, Royaumont, as a cultural center. But I didn't dare ask questions of people I hadn't met for fear of revealing my linguistic or cultural inadequacies. And what with my single-track Proustian preoccupation there didn't seem to be much grist to my mill there anyway.

Chapter 5

March 25 MME. SCHEIKÉVITCH came for lunch and in the afternoon took me to meet Céleste Albaret, Proust's housekeeper and guardian angel from 1913, when *Swann* was first published, to his death in 1922. Mme. S. had told me that her way of speaking was like her master's and that she now ran a small hotel. But she had given me no inkling of the grimness of the surroundings. Walking down the narrow little rue des Canettes, tucked in between the Place Saint-Sulpice and the Boulevard Saint-Germain, we arrived at a high narrow building, identified by a sign next to the door — Hôtel d'Alsace et Lorraine. *Bureau au 1ᵉʳ*.

We turned into a narrow, damp, stone passage into which no heat, light or air seems ever to have penetrated. The carved oak banister to which we clung going upstairs has fortunately withstood the wear and tear of centuries better than the steps. Some of them were merely split across. Others had whole boards trampled out by the heavy boots of poor working men, the only residents one could imagine in such a hotel.

We knocked on the flimsy, windowed door that led into the tiny crowded *bureau,* with its single high window from which a dark courtyard and the neighboring roofs are visible. A golden-oak roll-top desk stands against one wall and over it hangs a small board for keys and a larger one with tiny electric light bulbs that twinkle each time a lodger turns his light on or off. There were some mail-boxes and a small table with a vase of roses and a large ashtray advertising Pernod. But the out-standing object seeming to stretch the limits of this cold little room is a monstrous reproduction Boulle cabinet, the overhang of which juts out at an angle that would crack the skull of anyone rising from the only upholstered chair. The cabinet had be-longed to Proust, Mme. S. told me, and above it hung a landscape in musty oils painted in the early '90s by Paul Baignères, a friend of Proust's youth. We barely had time to glance around the *bureau* when the door to the next room opened and a very tall woman in a black dress and sweater came out to greet us.

It is difficult for me to describe Céleste because for the first time I found myself emotionally in-volved, acutely conscious of *le temps perdu.* I can't remember her face as well as the beauty of her voice, the elegance of her speech, the rhythm of her long, long sentences which never dragged to an end but seemed always to achieve a carefully composed climax. Her bearing as she stood in the doorway to the small adjacent room was as striking as her speech. Proust described her as a "Jeanne d'Arc Recamier Botticelli." Now, in her late fifties, traces of what he saw there are still discernible. But primarily the impression she made on me was that of a natural *grande dame* whose stature rises above any surroundings.

It was an honor, she said, to receive someone who had come so far in order to do homage to her master. She had already been told, she said, of the quality of my scholarship, although she, of course, was a humble working woman who had always lacked both the time and the intelligence to read books. Nevertheless anything she could tell me to help me would be act of love for the memory of M. Proust who, she assured me, was never long out of her thoughts. And if I would honor her poor table by accepting a cup of tea, et cetera, et cetera . . . But one cannot reproduce Céleste's speech without making it sound falsely artificial — an inaccurate and wrong impression. There is artifice in her words, but it is the artifice of poetry. Her "language," Proust wrote in his novel, "was somehow so literary that . . . one would have thought her speech affected." And he wrote, too, of "her curious genius," saying that Albertine's "wealth of poetry" was "less strange, less personal than that of Céleste Albaret."

Nothing could be more "personal" during this dreadful cold winter when there is no tea in Paris than for Céleste to have decided not only that it was correct to offer an American lady afternoon tea rather than coffee, but actually to spare the time and money to go to a black market to procure the tea. Not until she poured it did I notice that her fingernails were literally worn down to the quick.

One reads about such hard-worked hands, but to see them on such a person was painful indeed.

The table was set in a windowless room which serves as dining room, kitchen, bedroom and salon. A large white iron bed stands in one corner with a crucifix on the wall above it. Along other walls there are a coal stove, a meager sink with its single cold water tap and a cupboard for dishes and pots and pans.

Most of the space in the small room is occupied by the dining table and five excessively uncomfortable straight-backed chairs. There is barely space to move around. But the room was warm — warm enough so that I could actually take off my coat without freezing. Additional warmth entered the room with the appearance of Odilon Albaret, Céleste's husband — a title he vociferously deplores and out of which stem endless angry marital arguments. Odilon had come home early from the bistro proudly to do honor to the guests. He soon made it clear that having been Marcel Proust's chauffeur from 1907 to the time of his death, he was a familiar of the master many years before Céleste, who entered his service only after their marriage in 1913 at the age of twenty-two.

Odilon is a short, ruddy, plump little man whose seventy years are well hidden, but whose clipped, rather military-looking mustache does not disguise his essentially peasant quality. His speech, Mme. S. told me, intrinsically rather rough and ready, slurs so completely, after a few glasses of wine, into the *patois* of his native province that even to a Frenchman it becomes incomprehensible, except for certain universal monosyllables.

Just what Céleste was saying about Proust when a knock came on the door, I can't remember. The interruption was caused by a very small, very wrinkled nun who, dressed in the habit of a nursing sister, stood in the doorway. *"Entrez, ma soeur, entrez."* Céleste was all gentleness and welcome; and while Odilon leaped for a chair and another cup, Céleste explained to me that the good sister came from Aurillac, her own birthplace in the Lozère. To the sister she merely said that Madame had come all the way from *les Etats-Unis,* and we were talking about Marcel Proust.

"Marcel Proust?" the nun repeated blankly.

"C'était un homme de lettres," Céleste explained.

All the time I was at Céleste's I kept thinking how impossible it was to imagine Proust's physical presence in these poverty-stricken surroundings. Yet it was the first time since I have been here that I had a real sense of the man himself, the artist. It was like a kind of magic. I shall certainly try to see Céleste as often as possible.

2

March 27   Jenny Bradley, to whom I feel closer every day, came for dinner and we went to see two much-touted Sartre plays. I suppose *Les mains sales* is important but it seemed to me interminable and indeterminate. *La putain respectueuse,* which I gather is supposed to be a serious commentary on American life, is the ultimate nonsense. How anyone who had ever been in the U.S. could think that was a valid treatment of the Negro problem I wouldn't know. His characters are just like the stereotypes of Frenchmen American playwrights used to put in those ridiculous eighteenth- and nineteenth-century farces that I read before giving my disastrous course in the American theatre at the New School. I haven't forgotten my feelings as the class dropped gradually from twenty-two to six.

March 30 Today I received a reply to the note I wrote the Prince Bibesco some three weeks ago. It was written on a tiny piece of paper and started halfway down the page. "Dear Mrs. Curtiss, Telephone me. Bibesco." His manners appear to be a variation of the Princesse Marthe's. In a postscript he asked whether I was related to the collector. What collector he meant I can't imagine. The only one I ever heard of was Henry James' and Mrs. [Isabella Stewart] Gardner's friend, Ralph Curtis, who lived in Venice and must have died years ago.

At first I was tempted to wait a few days before telephoning. But then I decided my job was more important than my pride so I called. He answered and I spoke French at first but he said in English, "Is this Mrs. Curtiss?" I said I was and then he asked whether I was related to the collector. I said no and there was a silence. So then he asked whether I had written much and I said nothing he was likely to know about. So then he said what did I do. So I said that I was a professor at a college called Smith. *"Ah, mais c'est pour les jeunes filles. C'est très chic."* He said he was very busy so I said that I didn't in the least wish to impose on him, that if he was too busy to see me, etc.

He then started to explain that he was having a play produced tonight but I interrupted and said I supposed he must be spending most of his time at rehearsals. He then asked how I knew Harold Nicolson and I said that he used to stay with me quite often when he was writing the life of Dwight Morrow, a job which I had secured for him. "Ah, the Morgan partner," he said. "They are friends of yours?" I said yes, so then he said that any friend of Harold's certainly came well recommended and would I telephone him soon to make an appointment.

When I asked Céleste about the Prince, she said he was *fou* and *mal-élevé*. But I must see him because he had been one of the first people to believe in M. Proust's work and M. Proust was fond of him even though the one to whom he was really devoted was his brother, Prince Emmanuel, who hanged himself because he thought he had syphilis which he really didn't have.

March 31 At last it looks as though I might be able to start the work I most want to do — read Proust's family letters and examine at least superficially his manuscripts and *cahiers*. They belong to his heir, Mme. Suzy Mante, the daughter of his brother, Dr. Robert Proust, a very successful surgeon. Her husband died shortly before I arrived so it seemed only decent to wait a month to get in touch with her. But today, after innumerable telephone conversations, she came to lunch with me in chic Balenciaga mourning. At first she told me of the details of her husband's death, her insomnia, her inability to eat, the depth of her grief, etc., etc. But eventually she talked about *"ce cher Marcel qui rassemblait tant à papa."* I couldn't but be amused by this concept. For although as brothers, Marcel and Robert undoubtedly had warm family feelings for each other, temperamentally as artist and scientist they could hardly have differed more.

Mme. Mante is cultivated and charming, slightly Semitic-looking which is odd as her father was only half Jewish and her mother not at all. Because of her Proustian connection it is difficult to characterize her at a first meeting. I cannot place her either in Swann's or the Guermantes' way. Indeed I can more easily picture her in a Balzac novel. She is shrewd, intelligent, and knowledgeable, and has promised to let me come to her house to see her uncle's manuscripts, etc., next Wednesday. But she may well change her mind. It is the inevitable amateur approach that gets me down.

I have gathered so much useful material over tea tables that I can't take notes on and that stews around inside me until I can remember it and write it down that I feel like a stuffed goose.

April 1   I have had a most delightful *poisson d'Avril,* the French April Fools' Day gift. It was a quite unpredictable Proustian gathering. Mme. Scheikévitch arranged a week ago to bring in at 4:30 today the Marquis de Lauris, one of Proust's oldest friends. Beautiful, tall, slender, starry-blue-eyed, gracious, gentle, certainly a model for St.-Loup's most endearing side. He's not frightfully quick-witted but wonderfully charming. He speaks no English but purely by accident we fell into an immediate rapport. I asked him how he had broken his leg the time that Marcel had so breathlessly climbed all those flights of stairs to see him. He was quite bowled over. How could I know about a detail like that? It seemed impossible. I was forced to admit I read Marcel's account of the visit in a letter to one of his other friends. What seemed like a silly question couldn't have been more *à propos*. For M. de Lauris is in the process of preparing Proust's letters to him for publication and he will let me see them and choose the ones I want.

At this point in our conversation, the Duchesse de Clermont-Tonnerre suddenly knocked on the door, as unannounced by the concierge as I had been when I called the Princesse Bibesco. But she had telephoned this morning to say that she was coming to the Ritz for tea and could she stop by and see me at about seven. I thought, of course, that the others would be gone by then — I simply can't remember what they say if I see more than one, or at most two, at a time — but the other guests stayed on and on and eventually the Duchesse appeared, looking for all her seventy or more years like a trim little terrier, done up in a smart tan *tailleur,* about the color of her hair, and a snappy red-fox jacket. She is extremely nearsighted, so I was put in the ridiculous position — me, the outsider — of introducing her to two people she has known for years. I knew that until she had extracted from her bag the single lorgnette she peers through she wouldn't recognize them and it would have been embarrassing for all. But it was old home week instead. The Duchesse was a little condescending to Mme. S., whom I think she had quite forgotten. But she made an enchanting pass at M. de Lauris whom she deplored not having seen for so long. They talked a little about dear Marcel and then on discovering that they live in the same *quartier* they went to dinner together. I was thus left to console poor Mme. Scheikévitch, who had, after all, every reason to believe that the Marquis would escort her home. But she wasn't at all bitchy about it. She just said how wonderfully chic and clever Mme. de C-T was and then started talking about when she would have to go to an old ladies' home and the four wounds on her breast where she tried to kill herself when she was twenty. She is poor and miserable and kind and generous but after a while it becomes tiresome, with the best will in the world, to listen to her, and wearing to extract Proustian data from all this stream of misery. But I sat her by the wood fire, fed her a large dinner and read out loud to her that funny piece of Harold Nicolson's in *Some People* — "The Marquis de Chaumont," based on Etienne de Beaumont, whom she knew.

3

April 5   I had a very congenial dinner with George Balanchine last night. He is suffering the same kind of frustration I am at French laziness and inefficiency. I've got more or less used to a four-day week, a four-hour day, and half my work done over the tea table. If I work more than two hours at a time in the unheated and unlighted library I develop such chills, headache and sinus that all I can do the rest of the day is come home, soak myself in brandy and aspirin and go to bed. George swears that he has at most a two-hour working day twice a week. The *corps de ballet* has only one full rehearsal a week and this week they're not having any because of the holidays. The *régisseur,* like the director of the library, is never available without an appointment and George can't get any scores at all to plan ballets, not even some Bizet he wanted. Then [Serge] Lifar has left a corps of saboteurs and he doubts whether he will get even two new ballets done in the six months he is here. However, they are making beautiful new costumes for *Sérénade,* the first of George's ballets to be given here. The Opéra must be difficult enough to work with in ordinary times but now in all this insecurity and general atmosphere of death by in-anition leading to death by violence, it's enough to try the patience even of amateurs and lovers of Paris. But for professionals to whom a city is, after all, merely a background for work, the complete lack of any sense of the importance of time, the ex-cessive *politesse* with which people promise things they never do, is enough to drive one mad.

April 12   It is certainly lucky that I decided to write this diary. Otherwise twenty years from now I would think that this whole last week when I failed to keep it was an hallucination — that I fancied my-self a recently discovered unpublished character in *Swann.* This witty, charming, scholarly Mrs. C., about whom all of Proust's friends telephone each other after they have met her and then telephone her to repeat what the others have said, I find an unrecognizable *alter ego.* But I don't suppose I am any more schizophrenic than before. After all, the private life of Professor Curtiss of the Smith College English Department was far from typically academic. Perhaps professionally I am a chameleon, taking on the color of whatever job I am doing. But the requisites for finding some unpublished letters of Proust, gathering information for footnotes for my book, were wholly unpredictable.

I suppose that twenty-five years ago my Bloomsbury adventure was equally exciting, but I was too young to have any detachment. And it would never have occurred to me to keep a diary about it. If it weren't for David's letters over the years and the portrait Duncan [Grant] painted of me, that time in London would seem like an intermittent kaleidoscope. My impression that they treated me much as their eighteenth-century forebears welcomed the "noble savage" is probably a literary fantasy. But, of course, I wasn't working then so there was no focus except being in love with David. Now the intensity is part of the job — passion not for people as individuals but for the part they may or may not have played in the creation of Proust's macrocosm, a world which has for so long been part of my own.

The week started with two visits to the American Hospital. The vile weather, the damp, cold hours working in the B.N. gave me such a miserable sinus attack I could hardly breathe. But penicillin inhalations given by a terribly nice American Doctor Bayon from Louisiana helped enough so that I was able to keep appointments I couldn't bear to have missed.

At 11:30 Wednesday morning I went to see M. Daniel Halévy. He lives in an eighteenth-century house on the Quai de l'Horloge, just the other side of the Pont Neuf. The house is not impressive and there was no formality. The concierge simply told me to go upstairs and knock on the first door to the left. M. Halévy let me in to his study, which made me feel as though I had stepped into an earlier world. The small crowded room with its view of the Seine contained a couch-bed, a huge desk, an armchair covered in the same faded amber velvet I remember in the Beacon Hill houses from the Boston of my youth. Books were scattered everywhere and my eyes popped out of my head at the Degas drawings on the wall. The family portraits were by Jacques-Emile Blanche, and M. Halévy himself, with his full beard, his long hair, his sensitive intellectual face, his bright, inquiring eyes, looked as though he had stepped out of one of Nadar's marvelous photographs.

M. Halévy is the only person I was really frightened of meeting. A distinguished historian, the first real scholar I have met, whose path rarely crossed Proust's after they left the university — what business did I have encroaching on his time to ask an important favor. This was the only encounter for which I prepared carefully. I took along my books, marked in the places I needed information. M. Halévy is not given to small talk. The usual compliments and *politesses* would have been supererogatory. So I showed him a letter I had marked that Proust wrote to a schoolmate when he was fifteen. "Are you trying to tell me that Halévy thinks I am raving mad . . . insufferable, that my eagerness to see him — sage that he is — at first ridiculous, and very soon tiresome; that he wanted me to feel that I was too clinging and wished to be rid of me?"

"You were very severe with him, weren't you?"
I said. "Worse than that — harsh, even ruthless."
His beautiful English helped me to relax. I explained that what I most needed was to see his
aunt Mme. Straus' letters from Proust. I knew
the published edition was bowdlerized and garbled
and I wanted the translation to include the deleted
proper names and other passages.

Unfortunately, he said, he did not own and had
never seen the original letters. But he did have the
proof sheets with his own unpublished corrections.
He took them out of a carton, handed me a pad
and pencil and said he would dictate some deleted
passages. I was terrified. Unused to taking dicta-
tion even in English, I had no faith that I could
pass what was obviously some sort of test of my
ability. I lectured myself the way I had students
whose final exams would determine their gradua-
tion, and, by God, I passed. He then talked to me
about why he disliked Proust as a human being
while admitting his greatness as an artist. He explained that he did not have his aunt's actual letters
because of quarrels and a lawsuit he had lost in an
effort to keep her papers, as well as those of her
father and of her first husband, Georges Bizet, in
the family. Instead they went to the widow of her
second husband's nephew — a Mme. René Sibilat,
who is said to be mad.

Those two hours with M. Halévy were by far
the most valuable I have spent. It is faith-restoring
to deal with someone who as well as being charming and attractive takes for granted the need for
accuracy. Two days after I was there I had a note
from him saying that on going over the proofs again

he had found a penciled note of a sentence Proust had crossed out in letter XLVII which he had failed to notice and which might alter the meaning a little. Would I come in the A.M. on the 24th so he could show it to me. To Mme. Mante this would seem a very minor favor indeed. To me the postscript to M. Halévy's note — "Texts have their rights, too" — is what makes research so rewarding.

On Thursday M. Maurice Duplay came to call on me. I had never heard of him until I discovered by chance in a copy of the *Revue Nouvelle* a small batch of letters Proust had written him between 1905 and 1922. The son of a famous surgeon, a colleague of Proust's father, he was younger than Marcel. But the two families often spent their holidays together. It was clear from the letters that although Duplay's and Marcel's friendship almost dwindled away, they were warm although not intimate friends in the 1900s. M. Duplay was apparently for some years a more or less successful novelist. A dozen or more of his books are catalogued in the B.N., but none since 1936. I wanted to meet him because Proust's long letters praising and criticizing Duplay's books made him sound interesting. And in a way he was — not as an individual but because he is in such a different category from Proust's other friends I have met. He looks a little like a bourgeois version of Odilon — ruddy-faced with a small mustache. One might have met him in Mme. Verdurin's salon in the early days. He talked about his father's friendship with Proust's father and how little Dr. Proust understood his son — nothing new. But he very

graciously presented me with a copy of an unpublished letter of condolence Marcel had written him
when M. Duplay's mother died. It is so like other
letters I have already included that I can't use it.
But it was touching of him to bring it to me.

Chapter 6

April 12
(continued) THE GENTLE, POLITE M. Duplay was no preparation for Bibesco, who has been so boringly uncooperative, never willing to make a specific appointment, always saying to telephone him again. So I was really astonished Tuesday when I received a postcard with a picture of his beautiful house on the Ile St.-Louis, saying, "Come at twelve. Bibesco. I have been frantically busy with my play." This communication arrived at about twelve so I called him and said, "You don't mean today, do you?" Oh, no, he couldn't see me today. So I said, "Well, I couldn't see you today either. I'm still in bed." "Bed!" he cried with joy. "You're still in bed!" It was clear that I had found the password. "Were you up late last night?"

"No, I was ill and went to bed early."

"Well, tell me what it is you really want to see me about . . . This Proust book . . . how long will it be?"

"One hundred and fifty thousand words."

"Hmm . . . An important book, eh? Who's publishing it?"

"Proust's American publishers."

"Oh! My dear Mrs. Curtiss, I want you to say something nice in this book about Antoine Bibesco."

"I'd like to, but how can I if I never meet him?"

"But you will. You'll come and see me. When?"

"I'll come Friday at twelve."

"You will telephone me first?"

"No, I will not telephone you first. I've telephoned you all the times I'm going to. American women don't keep telephoning people."

"Listen — I have a better idea. You lunch with me Friday."

"Prince, you're being reckless. How do you know you'll like me enough to want to lunch with me? I'll come at twelve and if you don't like me I'll leave at one. If you do, I'll lunch with you."

"Tell me what you look like, what kind of woman you are."

"Oh, I'm a great amazon of a woman."

"Ah, I adore amazons. Are you divorced?"

"I'm a widow."

"How long?"

"Eighteen years."

"Children?"

"None."

"Ah, my dear Mrs. Curtiss, I do look forward to seeing you." And it turned out he really did. At quarter to twelve on Friday I telephoned and asked whether he was still expecting me. He was eagerly waiting. So over I went to the most heavenly house on the prow of the Ile St.-Louis, with a view of both sides of the Seine. The concierge's daughter showed me into a room so beautiful it took my breath away — full-length Vuillard panels obviously painted to fit on the walls, Degas drawings. It was all too much to try to look at quickly. I just tried to soak in the view and the wonderful light from both sides of the river reflected in the mirrors on the wall. As I stood looking out the window he came in. He is very handsome, typecast for a diplomat — tall, white-haired, with shrewd fox eyes, dressed in striped trousers and a morning coat. He stopped quite near me, put in his monocle, looked at me, and said, "But you should have told me in the first place that you're beautiful. You *are* beautiful. What lovely skin!" A finger down my cheek. "So soft! How clever of you not to use make-up . . . and your hands" — one of them in his, finger by finger — "so distinguished. None of that dreadful red paint . . . You must let me show you my house."

It took all my self-control not to burst into *fou rire* but I managed to make sensible comments about all of the beautiful rooms, each with its colossal bed or sofa. We finally sat down opposite each other before a wood fire in his bedroom. "Now I want to know all about you," he said. "Why do you work? You must be rich. You stay at the Ritz. Where did you get your money?" So for ten minutes I was catechized about my family, my husband, etc., etc.

"Are you a cold American?"

"That is something I'm afraid you'll have to find out for yourself, Prince." A hand on the knee at once. "I didn't mean this minute. After all, I did come to see your letters from Proust."

Up he jumped, put in my lap an album of all
P.'s letters to him and his brother Emmanuel. He
let me thumb through them so I could drool at
seeing how many there were, and then whisked
them away again.

"Now, you'll be sweet to me. Now you'll go to
bed with me. Look what a lovely bed it is."

"Perhaps I'll come some night and sleep with
you in it but not quite so soon, if you don't mind.
I've only been here twenty minutes."

"I know, I know. But look what you've done to
me. Give me your hand." At this point the *fou
rire* did *éclate.*

"I don't need tangible evidence. I can see. Besides, it's not the first time it's happened to me you
know."

"But darling, I thought I was impotent. I have
been for months. But you have roused me, you
marvelous amazon. Let me kiss your lips."

"My hand, if you like."

"No, if you won't give yourself to me we must
go out for lunch at once, otherwise I'll rape you."

"It takes two to make a successful rape, I have
always heard." So out to lunch we went.

On the rather long walk past the Hôtel de Ville
to a huge, noisy, commercial-type restaurant, he
asked me whether I had a lover in Paris, in London, in America. He is in love with a woman he
wants to marry but her husband won't die, so she
has gone away and God has sent me to console him
in his loneliness. How long since I had slept with
anyone? Four months. Ah, much too long. I
agreed. At lunch he was enchanting, intelligent,
sympathique, illuminating about Proust, altogether

delightful, except for one incident. He ordered sole *meunière* and when it was brought he disapproved of the way the waiter boned it and made a most outrageous, noisy scene which appalled me. I wanted to crawl under the table, and decided nothing would ever make me dine out with him again. Then, as though there had been no interruption, he asked whether I was religious, Catholic or Protestant? No, neither, not religious. I suspect the truth percolated through to his Rumanian anti-Semitism but what the hell. "You're not a cold American, are you? May I come to the Ritz tomorrow night?"

"Suppose you don't like me. Suppose I don't ever see you again. How do I know you'll show me Proust's letters? I want to see the letters first." No, *le plaisir* first, then the letters. I knew it was a gamble, but after all, I figured, the letters are unique and there are plenty of women who must like this kind of approach or he wouldn't have continued using it. He asked me how old I was and I told him. He asked me how old I thought he looked, and I said sixty. A little older, he said. I know that he's sixty-nine. We separated on a street corner and he said, "You're so cold, so distant. You haven't even given me a kiss." So I pecked his cheek and pursued my way to the rue d'Arcole through a flower market. Suddenly I felt arms around me, a kiss on the back of my neck and a voice in my ear, "Darling, let me come tonight. I can't wait until tomorrow." The flower-women and their offspring were all enchanted by this little scene of Parisian life. It would have made a perfect subject for a painting by Jean Béraud. But I was still seeing all those letters in my mind's eye so I said "yes," or maybe I just said "yes" because it has never been easy for me to say "no." If I had realized sooner that the Prince has always been an unsuccessful playwright I might have been better prepared for his theatrical approach to life.

After the rather Feydeauesque conclusion of this unusual variation of scholarly research I wanted to go back to the hotel and, if not actually collapse, at least consider the situation I've got myself involved in. But I couldn't. At three-thirty I had an appointment on the other side of Paris to meet another old friend of Proust's, Fernand Gregh.

2

The contrast between Antoine's princely residence on the Ile St.-Louis, all elegant, ancient stone, and the tree-shaded garden in Passy surrounding M. Gregh's belle époque version of a rustic country house was surprising. Hameau Boulainvilliers is the perfect place to harbor such turn-of-the-century poets as M. Gregh and his late neighbor Pierre Louÿs. It took a rapid personality change on my part to cope with the abrupt transition from the amorous prince to the gentle minor poet and would-be academician.

In spite of his impressive looks — tall, slender, long white beard, lots of white hair — I am afraid M. Gregh is rather a shallow man, but not unattractive and certainly not as silly as Mme. de Clermont-Tonnerre made him out. She claims he's the chief model for Bloch, which may have a slight tangential truth. But he is not a Jew. The only traits they noticeably share are vanity and ambition, as do many others. He is rather a figure of fun in the literary world because he fancies himself as a poet, has only occasionally published minor verse, while trying twelve or fourteen times to become a member of the Académie Française. But he doesn't act at all frustrated. He is, in fact, publishing his memoirs this year, so was delighted to talk about his youth and the pre–1914 war period.

As it was the first really warm spring day we have had, we sat under an umbrella in the garden, full of flowering bushes and hyacinths and tulips in bloom, and chatted. He has just recovered from the war — a lonely and anxious time for him. His wife, a Jewess, fled across the border to Spain just as the Germans started occupying Paris. Communication had been almost impossible and red tape had prevented her return until fairly recently. She, too, is a poet, he said, and still suffering the effects of her exile. That was why she asked to be excused from meeting me and serving tea. He is a great gossip but the only comments he made that stick in my mind are about M. Halévy. He said that Daniel was a disappointed, bitter man because his writings have never achieved the international success of his brother Elie's *History of England in the 19th Century* or of Marcel's books. I daresay there's a slight element of truth in this but he is certainly in no discernible way a warped human being. I suspect there is a slight jealousy in this judgment. In any case, my visit to M. Gregh was worthwhile. He loaned me typed copies of thirty-five unpublished letters Proust had written him.

Not only was it a generous gesture but it freed me from the always exhausting labor of deciphering that difficult handwriting. My eyes are perpetually tired.

That evening as I was sitting in my salon reading the Gregh letters the Prince arrived on the dot of nine-thirty as he said he would. "But you're not in bed," he complained. "All afternoon I've been picturing walking in and finding you waiting for me in bed." I protested at this, offered him a brandy and soda, a cigarette. "I'm not one of your Englishmen or Americans. I don't drink though I own vineyards in Rumania and I don't smoke. I want you. I wrote you a love letter this afternoon. You will have it tomorrow morning."

I must hand it to the Rumanians. Their idea of impotence in old age is the Anglo-Saxon notion of potency in the prime of life. And afterward he was delightful. *Enfin* to talk about Proust in a horizontal position was as relaxing, as useful as the thought of his ghost in the room was amusing. Antoine intends publishing the letters so I told him I would date them for him and sell a *choix* to *The Atlantic Monthly*. And with all due respect to the sudden inflation value of my physical gifts I am inclined to think that his real taste and knowledge and his need for money will, in the long run, be the deciding factors as to who comes out victorious in this little game. How long the run will be is a question that bothers me a little. I leave for London three weeks from tomorrow.

As he left he stopped, made the sign of the Cross over me and said, "Do you like peppermints?" Being unfamiliar with the rites of the Greek Orthodox

Church I was puzzled and replied, "Are they strong?" "Oh, no, very mild." Sweets in Paris are as rare and costly as Bourbon whiskey was last summer at home. He pulled a package out of his coat pocket, opened it and produced several little cellophane bags of poison green peppermints. He put two down on the mantel. A horrid phrase ran through my mind — two bits on the mantelpiece. "One is plenty," I said.

"I'll be back Tuesday night," he announced. "I shall sleep here then." He uses the royal *we* when expressing opinions. "We think . . . etc." But about *l'amour* he speaks as an individual.

"You had better telephone me," I said. "I might be too tired." And I well might be, for that is the day I go to Mme. Mante's.

The "love" letter duly arrived, enclosed in a piece of paper that said, "Dearest, I am enclosing a 'love' letter. Antoine." It certainly needed labeling. It was a plan of attack, described in detail in the most clinical and exact language. I really was outraged; it was so appalling. But then I had to laugh. The action had been carried out so exactly according to plan . . . Besides it's rather chic that the first person who ever *tutoied* me is a Prince. "From a merchant's daughter to the Guermantes way, that's quite a journey," he said. Which of us will outwit the other is an open question.

3

April 14   Céleste telephoned, making a long, splendid, Proust-style speech, the import of which was that she had thought of a person who could be helpful to me and would I honor her by stopping by in the afternoon so she could tell me about him. During my visit our conversation was frequently interrupted by the intrusion of what appeared to be Czech or Jugo-Slav workingmen, her tenants, who looked for their mail. But eventually she came to the point. "I should not wish to press anybody's presence on Madame," she said, "but M. le Docteur Le Masle I am sure Madame would like. *Il est vraiment homme du monde, Madame, il parle anglais et il est toujours si gentil pour moi."* I assured Céleste I should be delighted to meet any friend of hers, but had M. le Docteur known M. Proust? No, but he had studied medicine under M. le Docteur Robert Proust, Marcel's brother, and had written a little book about Dr. Adrien Proust, father of the two brothers. So it was arranged that Dr. Le Masle and I should meet there for lunch on Friday.

I told Céleste of Antoine's reluctance to show me her master's letters, sparing her the ridiculous details. "You must not stop trying," she said. "M. Proust from time to time would be very angry at Prince Antoine. But they always remained friends. M. Proust once said to me, *'Antoine est un sauvage, mais d'ailleurs, un sauvage intelligent. En Roumanie il a une grande proprieté avec beaucoup d'esclaves et il pense qu'il peut traiter tout le monde comme si eux aussi étaient des esclaves.' "* [Antoine is a barbarian, but an intelligent one. In Rumania he owns a large estate with lots of serfs and he thinks he can treat everybody as if they too were serfs.]

I told Céleste I was lunching with Mme. Mante tomorrow and asked what she thought of Proust's niece. Céleste said she had not seen her since

Proust's funeral. He had rarely been well enough to receive Suzy, but had worried that the title of *Sodome et Gomorrhe* might somehow reflect on the reputation of the eighteen-year-old girl for whom he felt a certain family sentiment. I decided it would be wise not to mention to Mme. Mante my friendship with her uncle's housekeeper.

April 15   Such a disappointment! Having at last been invited to breach Mme. Mante's stronghold I hoped this luncheon would lead her to letting me come each day for a few hours to work on the letters she has and to choose illustrations from the family photographs. From the moment I entered her large, richly furnished house in Neuilly, I realized what an optimistic idiot I am. On a large table in a luxurious salon lay three great volumes of the manuscript of *A la recherche* — no letters, no *carnets*, no photographs. Over the mantel hangs the Jacques-Emile Blanche portrait of Proust as a pasty-faced shallow dandy. Blanche's lifelong ambivalence about Proust, the characteristic malice in his descriptions of Marcel in his books, are clearly responsible for this false image which is after a fashion a self-portrait of Blanche. Such a pity that this near caricature is the most widely reproduced portrait of Proust. Instead of being glad to see the original it just made me angry. I kept comparing it to the rarely reproduced drawing made at about the same time with Proust, similarly dressed, *boutonnière* and all, that is a true portrait of the artist as a young man.

As usual, I was prompt, a social defect in New York and Paris where no one expects you to be on time. But I seem unable to break myself of this wasteful habit, a hangover from my recurrent night-mare when I was teaching. I would arrive at class eleven minutes late, just in time to see the students snaking off down the corridor after waiting the required ten. Although this disaster never happened except in my sleep, the latent fear was sufficiently traumatic to result in my always being an inconveniently early guest. While I waited for Mme. Mante to appear I dared to touch the opening page of *Swann* and felt an emotion as close to religion as I am likely to experience.

After about fifteen minutes Mme. Mante entered, demonstratively cordial, vociferously welcoming, full of excuses for not having received me sooner. I spoke of the thrill I felt at seeing and touching her uncle's manuscripts. She thereupon said she had been unable to find time to go through the letters and photographs; that indeed, with all the demands on her for the settlement of her husband's estate, she couldn't say when she'd be free to do it. I wanted to scream. I wanted to turn and leave. Instead we went in to lunch joined by her two teenage daughters. I don't remember the subject of our conversation except that she told me that next week she was seeing Antoine, whom she had not seen in years. He had persuaded her to see him by saying that he knew she was receiving his great friend, Mrs. Curtiss.

After lunch I was allowed to glance through the manuscripts while Mme. Mante chatted with me. My frustration was slightly diminished by her declaration of affection for me and her desire to see me as often as possible. Nevertheless my supply of charm to barter for letters is rapidly dwindling.

4

April 18   Lunch at Céleste's to meet Le Masle. Wonderful
food. He is an engaging, attractive person, quite
beautiful to look at in a curious way. Slender, dark-
haired, with deep-set black eyes that are rather
frightening — drugs or some element of madness
— sympathetic and personal in the way so many
homosexuals are. He couldn't be more Proustian
both literally and figuratively. He studied medicine
under Marcel's younger brother, Robert, and is the
author of a helpful little monograph on their father,
Dr. Adrien Proust. Although he served in the
British army and has a passion for Americans, I
somehow felt that he might have stepped out of
the pages of *Sodome et Gomorrhe*. With all his
charm and intelligence there is something warped
about him. I doubt whether I would have had this
impression of deviousness at a first meeting if it
weren't for Céleste's discreet replies to my questions
after he had left. I couldn't tell whether he's ever
practiced medicine or whether he has been dis-
barred. *"Alcool"* is his problem, Céleste said, and
a difficult, more or less invalid mother. I suspect
drugs as well as alcohol, but I shall be able to tell
more about him after our expedition to Illiers on
Sunday. It was essential for me to see the original
of M. Proust's Combray, he explained to Céleste,
who has never read the book. As she had never
been there either, I suggested that we three drive
there on Sunday.

April 19   No progress in my efforts to see the Bibesco letters.
Not that the Prince hasn't tried to maintain our

"affair," if such it can be termed, on the same high and noble level on which it started. I have been pelted with daily telephonings, telegrams, *petits bleus,* flowers and his variety of "love" letter. One of them made me so angry that I answered with a masterpiece of invective which produced the flowers and the following typical example of his non-amorous epistolary approach: *"Je suis un peu souffrant et neurasthénique — a contribué à ma neurasthénie le mauvais traitement que vous m'avez fait subir. Dès que j'irai bien, je vous téléphonerai. A."* Enchanted by this typical nonsense, I telephoned him only to find, of course, that he had gone out. He was lunching with Mme. Mante. After the lunch he called me to say that he was still *souffrant* and that she had spoken beautifully of me.

The issue between us is simple enough. He wishes only to come and see me at ten o'clock at night and I won't receive him at any time until he has shown me the letters. At first, I invited him to dinner but he always refused. I think he went every night to his play, which closed down this week. It was a failure of no mean proportions, though I am told it wasn't as bad as the critics say. That, of course, is the real cause of his *"neurasthénie."* He is immensely jealous of Sartre's success, and perhaps his feelings really were hurt when I ended my protesting letter by saying that if he didn't stop assuming he could treat me *en putain respectueuse* I would never see him again. Whether he can be enticed into showing me the letters remains to be seen.

Chapter 7

April 20 ILLIERS WITH Céleste and Robert Le Masle. So many impressions and ideas, relevant and irrelevant, I had better set them down on paper before they blend into a muddle.

Illiers, the actual little town, like so many others in France, bears somewhat the same relation to the Combray Proust's memory created as a variation on a theme in music to the basic structure of the work. Fortunately just before we started I read his opening description of Combray: ". . . these Combray streets exist in so remote a quarter of my memory, painted in colors so different from those in which the world is decked for me today, that in fact one and all of them, and the church which towered above them in the square, seem to me now more unsubstantial than the projections of my magic-lantern." Otherwise the shrinkage of Proust's magic Combray into a somber townscape — a pretty-enough public garden, a nice little brook-sized river, and a church less beautiful than his writing

about it — would have been a great disappointment.

The drive across the rich fields of the Beauce
was rather schizophrenic. The apple trees in bloom
made me temporarily homesick for my own orch-
ards. But to Céleste, city-eyed, they signified only
the recollection of the times when M. Proust would
suddenly send Odilon out in the country to fetch
a few branches of apple blossoms so that he could
look at them through a glass door without risking
an attack of asthma from the scent.

At Illiers we stopped at the family house and
were greeted by the Mesdames Bichot, two small
ladies of a certain or uncertain age, dressed all in
black. What kin they are to Proust I never discovered. They made no pretense of ever having
known him but listened enchanted to Céleste's
politesses and her accounts of their famous relative.
Le Masle seems to have a close enough relationship
with these humble ladies to use their house as a
storeroom. For just as we were about to leave, he
emerged carrying a huge painting by Suzanne
Valadon, whom I am ashamed to say I never heard
of. But she is a well-known painter, a friend of
Degas and the mother of Utrillo, whose widow is
a great friend of the doctor's. There is to be a
Valadon exhibition next week to which he is lend-
ing this picture or, I suspect, putting it up for sale.
He assumed that I wouldn't mind taking it to Paris.
How it was to be fitted into the car I couldn't see.
But by leaving the trunk-door open and using a lot
of rope supplied by the Mesdames Bichot, there
was room for Valadon's brilliantly colored women
to accompany us to Paris.

The conversation on the way back was fascinating. From casual chatter and jokes about Proust's friends, Céleste's wonderful mimicry of them, the talk would suddenly, without any transition, fall into her characteristic pattern of formal courtesy. Somehow she brought up the subject of French indifference to her master's work when it first appeared in contrast to British and American appreciation. She spoke of how happy it had made Proust to receive letters from abroad after the publication of *Swann's Way*, when at home not even his friends could be bothered to read this strange, difficult book. He had been particularly delighted with a letter from an English novelist whom he much admired. Could Céleste remember the writer's name? "Why yes, Madame, I think that it was a M. *Henri Jammes*."

"There was a Henry James," I said. Could Céleste remember what he had written M. Proust? But of course, Madame, she could. M. Proust often read her his letters.

M. Jammes had said that *Swann* was an extraordinary book for so young a man to have written; that it was a pity that Monsieur had lived too soon before his time. Because M. Jammes thought the subject matter was so difficult that not many people would understand or be interested in it. He said that he thought *Swann's Way* was the greatest French novel since *Chartreuse de Parme*, but he was afraid that M. Proust would perhaps suffer the same fate as Stendhal, of never being recognized in his lifetime.

This piece of information excited me so much that my impression of Illiers is already rather blurred. When I go back to London I must find out whether James' secretary remembers anything about the letter.

April 22 Mme. Scheikévitch came for tea. I haven't seen her for some time as she has been ill so I had to tell her about everybody I'd met in the meantime. Le Masle, she says, is a very dubious character, associates with Albert, the Jupien of the novel, and collects letters Proust is supposed to have written to various low-life types. Most of them are forgeries. He also wheedles things out of Céleste, such as Proust's bedroom curtains which he offered to store for her and his mother cut into bedspreads. I gather Céleste confided these things to Mme. S. but defended Robert as not being at fault in these matters and always so good to her.

When I told Mme. S. I had met Antoine she said he was a dreadful man, very unreliable. If he ever came to see me, she warned, I must be sure to put away all my letters and private papers. Otherwise he would try to read them if I left the room. When I confessed that reading other people's letters was also one of my weaknesses, she wouldn't believe me.

In the evening Antoine telephoned and when I told him of her warning he exploded in a rage. "Only servants do that," he said. "It's an insult. She doesn't like me. I never found her attractive."

I didn't tell him that we shared this vice for fear he might use the insult as an excuse for not showing me Marcel's letters.

2

April 24   A strange and fascinating day. At 11:30 I went back to M. Halévy's who greeted me with a whole folder of Proust's letters. After I left, he said, he looked through his files to see if there was anything I could use. He found things he had quite forgotten, hadn't had time to look at most of them. He handed me a letter Proust at seventeen had written to the fifteen-year-old Daniel. The first four pages were literary, about books, etc. Then the tone changed to a rather graphic description of the aesthetics of his seduction of a younger boy. After a page or so I stopped to ask M. Halévy whether he had read the letter. He had only glanced at it. "It seemed to be literary. Isn't it?"

"My dear M. Halévy," I said, in what I now realize was my school-marm voice, "you really shouldn't trust strangers so much. I am a reliable person. And, of course, there is no danger of this letter ever being published because Mme. Mante wouldn't permit it. But some unscrupulous person could copy it, paraphrase it in a book, which would be very unpleasant for you."

I handed him the homosexual pages. He read a few sentences and said, "*Vous avez raison, Madame.* But at least I was right in judging you as trustworthy."

In the afternoon I went to see M. Gregh, who was very gracious about my not including any of his letters in my book. Actually they weren't very interesting, but I gave as my excuse their duplication of material I had already translated. He presented me with a copy of his poem, *Rêverie à Central Park* — a paperbound limited edition of 1200 copies published by Brentano's. I have read only enough of this long work to see why he is considered such a minor poet. After I got home I discovered he had written it in New York in 1938. But as he gave it to me as I was leaving I had no opportunity to ask him about his visit there. His *dédicace* is so overwhelming I am going to copy it here. I might easily lose the book in my travels but I cherish the flattery of *"A Madame Curtiss, grande Proustienne — un poète admirateur de l'Amérique avec ses respects charmés"* — and a splendid long tail on the "h" of the signature.

3

April 28

Only a week left in Paris. No time to keep this diary — too busy copying letters and persuading photographers to reproduce faded old pictures. Forced to see people like Robert Le Masle whose half-true low-life gossip is no use to me and unable to find time for Jenny Bradley who is the one true friend I have made here and can only talk to on the telephone. The real trouble that made me feel I must stop Proustifying was the realization that I can't meet my deadline. It will take more than six months to do the notes and improve the translation and I am determined not to publish the book without some of Antoine's letters and a few of Proust's early letters to his mother.

Just as I was about to fall into one of my awful depressions the Huxleys rescued me with a totally non-Proustian weekend. Juliet telephoned on Friday to say they were going to Les Andelys in Normandy for the weekend with a charming American — would I join them? Would I! — even though it made me feel guilty about canceling an appointment with the actress Louisa de Mornand. But I excuse myself by doubting whether I could believe anything she'd say anyway.

Les Andelys was lovely. The little inn was on the river bank and behind it stood the splendid ruins of Richard Coeur de Lion's castle. We sat out on the terrace for hours watching the barges go by with children playing, families eating, wash hanging out on deck. I literally soaked up the peace. No one could be more charming, natural and spontaneous than Juliet, and Julian's conversation, his sense of humor, are a joy. The American turned out to be John Marshall, an old friend of my brothers' whom I never happened to meet. He is with the Rockefeller Foundation and is in Paris on UNESCO business. He is handsome in the Anthony Eden style and very nice. If only we had met sooner he would have introduced me to Julien Cain, the director of the B.N., a *"relation"* that would have saved me yards of red tape and hours of work. But he said he would arrange for me to meet him next year. His assumption that I would be coming back made me face the fact that there is no alternative. The very thought of waiting until next year to see Antoine's and Suzy Mante's letters, of postponing my deadline, fussing with publishers threw me back into the depression that the good company, the delightful place, the sunshine and the country air had dissolved. But an enchanting

piece of live poetry that happened on the drive back
to Paris restored my spirits. We stopped at a place
Julian apparently knew well — a grove, fragrant
with wild lilies of the valley, that led into a wood
where the trees were alive with song. One or two
nightingales I have occasionally heard in the English countryside. But here a whole chorus of them
was singing divinely. To differentiate their songs
would never have occurred to me, but Julian, a
dedicated bird-watcher with a finely tuned ear for
music, compared their individual songs, pointing
out to us how many more notes than his fellows
one particular bird included in his song. All this
magic while Juliet and I picked great bunches of
lilies. Now my room is fragrant with their perfume
and I have regained the spirit I need to face this
last week coping with the Proustian cast of characters, old and new. In contrast to the woods, the
nightingales, and the wild flowers they seem theatrical indeed.

I went to see Jean-Louis Vaudoyer, M. Halévy's
brother-in-law. He is an art critic, formerly curator
of the Carnavalet. But all I knew about him was
that Proust, because he admired an article by Vaudoyer on the Vermeer exhibition at the Jeu de
Paume, asked him to go with him to see the *View
of Delft* — "the most beautiful picture in the
world." I had forgotten that V. is a balletomane,
the author of the scenario for Nijinsky's *Le Spectre
de la Rose*. However, he promptly reminded me,
saying that he had written another ballet scenario
which might interest my brother. I passed the
buck by pointing out that Balanchine was here in
Paris and his opinion would be more useful than
Lincoln's.

He is a tall, rather handsome man, much younger than the other friends of Proust I have met. Although he had nothing new to say about Proust he was very gracious and later sent me a copy of the excerpt about Vermeer from his article in *l'Opinion* that Proust praised. He also gave me a little book of Stendhal aphorisms he edited which I enjoyed reading as I crossed the Channel to London.

4

May 7   London. For once I have had common sense enough to make no engagements until tonight. All week I did so many things, saw so many people, I couldn't keep this diary at all. Yesterday when I left Paris, I was so tired I didn't think I could ever touch a typewriter again. But the crossing was smooth, the Golden Arrow is such a lovely train, the people at the Berkeley were so welcoming that, after a good night's sleep, I am ready to go to work again.

I left with far more peace of mind than I expected. Suzy Mante came twice for tea and once for dinner, urging me more wheedlingly each time to translate her uncle's letters to her grandmother. Considering that I find Proust's relationship with his mother one of the most painful aspects of his life, I was in no way tempted. But hopeful that she still might let me have a few of the letters for my book, I practiced the diplomacy I have learned from the French — in English one would call it plain hypocrisy. I said that I would love to do it but that it would take another year to finish the book I am doing and perhaps by then there might be someone else she would rather have. So the subject was left open and my diplomacy worked. The day before I left she came for tea and brought me copies of eight of Proust's letters to his mother and one to his grandmother. I forgive her all the anxiety she caused me, but wish I might have chosen the letters myself.

Antoine, too, crashed through after his fashion. I went to see him three weeks to a day after our only encounter, but this time he was a tamed savage, wholly amenable. Meeting me, he said, had made him decide to publish his letters from Proust. He had therefore been re-reading them for the first time since he received them and will send me copies to choose from as soon as he's read them all. But that moment is wholly unpredictable, as he doesn't want just a few of his letters to appear in English before the French publication he plans for next year. So perhaps by then I shall have won the battle.

I asked him whether he had really loved Marcel, and he said no, that it was his brother Emmanuel who had really cherished him. Antoine felt from the start that Marcel was a genius and after reading *Swann* he was convinced that Proust was the greatest of the geniuses he had known. The others were Anatole France and Vincent d'Indy, which only shows how fleeting is fame. Who today reads Anatole France outside of college French courses? Vincent d'Indy is remembered as a founder of the Schola Cantorum rather than as a composer. But d'Indy was a protégé of Antoine's mother, and France was the dean of writers when Proust appeared to be a frivolous dilettante. Some of Antoine's instincts are sound. He was very sweet and friendly and our previous encounter has begun to take on the form of fantasy.

Two experiences last week brought me in contact with Proust in a way that's hard to describe — material, tangible, and emotional, too. Certainly not intellectual. On Wednesday I went to see Jacques Guerin's Proust collection, which I didn't know existed until told by Monroe Wheeler, that peripatetic unofficial diplomat who was in Paris arranging for some sort of exhibition at the Museum of Modern Art in New York. Jacques Guerin, a rich man — Dorsay perfumes — is a very private person, dislikes the idea of showing his collection to anyone and is not partial to ladies. But he is a friend of Monroe's, who, always obliging, offered to introduce me to him at a cocktail party. He made no promises, however, as to the success of my mission. After the introduction I would be on my own. Fortunately for me M. Guerin's real passion for Proust, not just a collector's hobby, made it easy to break through his shyness. He has never met any of Proust's friends, so he listened with intense interest to accounts of my meetings with the Marquis, the Comte, the Duchesse, the Princesse, the Prince, and Céleste. He invited me to come to his house the next day.

It is a large house, facing the Parc Monceau, and as I entered the spacious foyer I was confronted with a wholly unexpected sight. In one corner, there appeared to be a kind of mock-up of Proust's bedroom, which indeed it was. There stood his bed, a huge bookcase, a large desk, and a chaise longue bearing, as if casually tossed there, the

famous *pelisse*, its fur collar mangy, the cloth worn
and oh, so sad! How M. Guerin acquired these
personal objects absolutely baffled me. But I didn't
dare ask, although he couldn't have been more
cordial and welcoming. The library into which he
led me is a splendidly proportioned room with
long windows giving a fine view of the park. Books,
cartons, and cases lined one wall. On the other
hung the pinkest of Pascin *putains* at one end, the
most blood-red of Soutine's sides of beef at the
other, and in between the greenest of Courbet
landscapes, with a waterfall. That aspect of Courbet's painting has never much appealed to me, but
the painting was perfectly hung to balance the
color in the other two pictures. In the salon another
surprise, this time joyful, confronted me. M. Guerin had laid out on the table a considerable number
of Proust's notebooks, all of which I thought Suzy
owned but didn't show me. The little *carnets* are
narrow — about four inches across and six or seven
inches long — and have amusing colored lithograph
covers of chic belle époque ladies and sporting
gentlemen. To finger through them was thrilling,
but what little of the text I was able to read appeared to be post–*Les plaisirs et les jours* and pre–
Swann. I would like to have spent hours looking
at them. But my appointment was at six, M.
Guerin had a dinner engagement at eight, and I
was going to the première of Georges Bizet's ballet
at the Opéra — no time to see half of what I
wanted. Paul Souday's first edition of *Swann* with
his marginal comments fascinated me. His stupid
journalistic criticism of the book upset Proust so
much that I was angry at Souday the whole time I

was translating Proust's letters to him. The more personal documents M. Guerin showed me were funny, sad, and distressing. There was a little note he wrote when he was about sixteen on a scrap of paper imploring his grandfather to send him a small sum of money to pay for a chamber-pot he had accidentally broken during his first visit to a bordello. He had been sent there by his father for what was termed a matter of "hygiene," a not uncommon practice among the *bourgeoisie* of the period.

M. Guerin showed me lots of other letters, both of Proust's and his mother's. There was no time to take notes, but one letter I do remember very well. It was clipped to what at first glance appeared to be a rather formal cabinet photograph of a group of three elegantly dressed, fashionably mustachioed young dandies — Robert de Flers, Lucien Daudet, and Marcel Proust. His mother wrote that she was horrified by the picture, that if it were displayed it would cause a scandal and she hoped he would destroy it. The tone of the letter certainly implies that she was aware of her son's homosexuality.

After reading Mme. Proust's letter I looked at the photograph more carefully and could see the quality that disturbed her. Marcel, heavily mustachioed, wearing a bow tie, a flower in his buttonhole and a cryptic smile on his face, is seated in front of Robert de Flers. The young playwright, with his small neat mustache, his hair *en brosse,* his bohemian-style loosely tied broad bow tie, hand in pocket, looks straight into the camera as if to show he were only accidentally present. In contrast, Lucien Daudet stands beside Marcel, his left arm bent at the elbow in a somewhat feminine gesture, the hand resting on his lapel, while his right elbow is resting on Marcel's shoulder, the hand, with curved little finger, on his friend's arm. Daudet's eyes appear to be almost closed as he gazes down at Marcel with an expression of infinite tenderness.

If it weren't for the episodes in *Swann* concerned with photographs I suppose Mme. Proust's letter might be differently interpreted. But the part poor M. Vinteuil's picture plays in his daughter's lesbian affair and the photograph of an actress *en travestie* found in the narrator's great-uncle's possession after his death, which became the source of Elstir's sketch of Odette as Miss Sacripant, do indicate a kind of sexual mystique about photographs. And indeed Mme. Proust herself belonged to the generation for whom photography was a novelty, the public display of which many people regarded as an invasion of privacy.

I left M. Guerin's house feeling hungry, as though I had barely tasted the hors d'oeuvres of a great feast. But he said I could come back next year and take all the notes I wanted.

The Saturday after I visited M. Guerin I lunched at Céleste's and met for the first time her and Odilon's daughter, Odile. If anything could make me believe in an immaculate conception it was that twenty-year-old girl. How blunt, hearty, red-faced Odilon could have ever begot a creature of such delicate beauty is incomprehensible. And even when she was Odile's age Céleste could not have had such finely chiseled features. Odile is not tall like her mother, but slender, beautifully built, with skin like a magnolia or camellia. Her greenish eyes, slanted a little in her oval face, her fine black hair rather formally arranged, evoke a slightly oriental quality, like a geisha in a Japanese print designed for the export trade. Her speech is as elegant as her mother's but quite different. Having been saturated with Proust worship all her life one feels that her clarity, her succinctness, may well be an unconscious rebellion against her mother's Proustian rhetoric. Outwardly there is no other sign of anything but devotion to her parents and unquestioning acceptance of her situation in life. She is a clerk in the town hall of the 6th *arrondissement,* not exactly an affluent neighborhood. To see this flower growing out of such crowded, impoverished surroundings makes you feel that although she was born several years after Proust's death, for Céleste she is his child-in-wish.

After lunch Robert Le Masle came and accompanied Céleste and me to Proust's grave. It was her idea that I should go. To me there has never been any emotional reward in going to the graves of people one has loved and lost. On the other hand, I have always enjoyed wandering along the tree-shaded, grassy paths of old New England cemeteries, admiring the sculpture on the tombstones and wondering about the life histories of those long-dead husbands and wives and their children.

The contrast between those country graveyards and Père Lachaise made my blood run cold. To reach Proust's grave we passed a number of large monuments in granite or stone, honoring the Czech, the Belgian, the Italian, the Greek soldiers *"morts pour la France"* in the 1914 war. I remembered Proust's letter about meeting one icy night two young American soldiers who asked him the way to the Hotel Bedford. They spoke no French and he no English but he managed to lead them to the hotel. He was moved by the thought, he wrote, that they came from "so far away." But that was a private personal feeling about two lost boys. No such emotion was induced in me by mediocre sculpture dedicated to hundreds or thousands of unknown soldiers. On the way to Proust's grave there was not one that could be described as "a fine and private place."

A thick, flat, simple, black marble tombstone, horizontally placed, marks the grave in which Proust and his parents are buried. A cross is carved into the face of the stone, and under the cross is the inscription "Marcel Proust, 1871–1922." On one of the narrower sides of the stone the names of his parents are inscribed. I asked Céleste whether Proust had often gone to his parents' grave. She ignored the question so I asked whether Proust had believed in any sort of religion. "I asked Monsieur that question," she said, "and he replied, 'Céleste, do you think that if I believed there was a realm where I could see *Maman* again I would have gone on living this terrible life I have lived?' "

Going to Père Lachaise seems to gratify Céleste. But in spite of my first shock at what earlier seemed to me the macabre exposure of Proust's private life in M. Guerin's foyer, I now realize that the sight of the bed in which he spent so much of his life, where *Swann* was created, the *pelisse* that warmed him summer and winter, evoked a far more personal emotion than that bleak grave in the famous cemetery.

Chapter 8

May 8

I DINED with Clive [Bell] last night — a predictably enjoyable evening. Two qualities make him delightful company — his wit and intelligence one takes for granted. But the other aspect of his charm is rarer. When you are with him you feel that you are the one woman in the world he has chosen to be with. This is a natural enough experience with lovers, but neither love, nor even necessarily affection, are essential to this situation. It springs, I think, from the man's basic attraction to women in general.

Bloomsbury has always been somewhat condescending about Clive, stigmatizing him as a "womanizer" which, they fail to realize, is quite different from a "lady-killer," who always has an eye out for the woman at the next table. Once he has maneuvered her into his domain her charm for him diminishes; and to reassure his ego he must again covet and conquer another unknown from the next table. Clive is not at all like that. The fact that he has been faithful to the mistress he has loved for many years in no way overshadows the illusion of his temporary companion's unique attraction. He says he is taxed with never resisting a bluestocking. "But they must be of blue silk" — such a nice form of flattery.

The only other man I have met who made me feel I was the one woman to whom he wanted to talk in a room full of people was Bertrand Russell. For fifteen minutes at a reception at President Neilson's house after Russell's lecture [at Smith College] years ago we sat together on a window seat and talked. About the conversation I remember nothing — only the lovely sensation of being singled out as irresistible by a very great man.

Clive reminded me of an amusing story from his little book on Proust. Antoine Bibesco criticized Marcel for speaking of "de Musset." It is not correct, Antoine explained, for the "de" in a title to stand first. You must say "Musset" or "Alfred de Musset" or "Monsieur de Musset." A few days later Antoine ran into Proust on the street on his way home from some sort of gathering. Were there any good pictures in the house where he had been, Antoine asked. "Nothing much," Proust replied, "except for a fine portrait by the painter you call Dyck." I had forgotten the anecdote read nearly twenty years ago, but I still remember the solace of Clive's inscription in the book, sent me as a message of condolence after Harry died. "For the unforgotten and unforgettable Mina," he wrote. That is how he always makes you feel even if you see him only once in ten years. It doesn't matter that his writing which seemed so *avant-garde* then has become dated with the years. He was one of the first critics to open the eyes of the British public to Matisse and Cézanne.

May 11   Sissinghurst with Harold and Vita today was heavenly. I knew the gardens would be wonderful but I hadn't pictured the ruins of the castle divided into separate houses. We hardly stayed indoors at all except for lunch at which there was a delicious salad I never had before — watercress, orange sections, chopped shallots, with a little orange juice in the lemon oil dressing. In another separate part of the castle was the drawing room with so many beautiful things that all I can remember is a kind of haze of mauve velvet, the sun shining on antique purple Venetian glass.

After lunch we walked through the gardens, some small and walled, others long and open, and everywhere more kinds of bulbs and flowering bushes than I ever dreamed of. I was so filled with envy that I can only remember one glorious *allée* which particularly struck me as I could perfectly well have thought of making one like it at home. On either side there is a long row of American white birches, so much whiter than the European birch. Vita saw our variety for the first time when she came to Ashfield fourteen years ago and promptly had sent to England what must be at least a hundred trees. In between the two rows of trees a space about twenty feet wide is a carpet of blue primroses, every shade from deepest purple to palest sky blue. I never even knew there were blue primroses, so I was grateful for an interruption which gave me time to absorb them by myself.

The interruption was the arrival of a huge container of live trout wheeled down by a gardener to the shore of the nearby lake. Vita directed Harold and the gardener in the rather complicated process of releasing the trout.

How much nicer Harold is as host and assistant gardener than as urban M.P. "The Peter Pan of diplomats," Lincoln and I used to call him, and the other night Clive described him as a "middle-aged, fifth-form boy." But he was very kind and helpful — let me copy two entries in his diary about meetings with Proust in 1919 during the peace conference in Paris.

Afterthought, 1977

Because Harold's book *Peacemaking 1919,* which includes his diary while a member of the British staff at the peace conference, has not been reprinted, I am including these two entries here. They reveal sharply so many basic traits of both Proust's and Harold's character.

"Mar. 2, 1919 ... Dine with Princess Soutzo [later Mme. Paul Morand] at the Ritz — a swell affair ... Proust is white, unshaven, grubby, slip-faced. He puts his fur coat on afterwards and sits hunched there in white kid gloves. Two cups of black coffee he has, with chunks of sugar. Yet in his talk there is no affectation. He asks me questions. Will I please tell him how the Committees work. I say, 'Well we generally meet at 10.0, there are secretaries behind ...' *'Mais non, mais non, vous allez trop vite. Recommencez. Vous prenez la voiture de la Délégation. Vous descendez au Quai d'Orsay. Vous montez l'escalier. Vous entrez dans la Salle. Et alors? Précisez, mon cher, précisez.'* So I tell him everything. The sham cordiality of it all: the handshakes: the maps: the rustle of papers: the tea in the next room: the macaroons. He listens enthralled, interrupting from time to time — '*Mais précisez, mon cher monsieur, n'allez pas trop vite.*' "

"April 30, 1919 . . . Dine with Jean de Gaigneron at the Ritz. Gladys Deacon [future Duchess of Marlborough] there. Very Attic. Also Marcel Proust. Very Hebrew. Sit next him. He asks more questions. I am amused by this. I suggest to him that the passion for detail is a sign of the literary temperament. This hurts his feelings. He says '*Non pas!*' quite abruptly and then blows a sort of adulatory kiss across the table at Gladys Deacon. But he soothes down again later. We discuss inversion. Whether it is a matter of glands or nerves. He says it is a matter of habit. I say 'surely not.' He says, 'No, — that was silly of me — what I meant was that it was a matter of delicacy.' He is not very intelligent on the subject."

It is only fair to Harold's memory to point out that *Sodome et Gomorrhe* was as yet unpublished.

May 11 (continued)   Vita paid me a compliment which touched me very much. She took me up into the tower which is her study and inviolable, she said, except to the very few friends she invites there. I remember vividly my surprise at her bread-and-butter letter after she and Harold stayed with me during their lecture tour all those years ago. She wrote that she numbered me among her friends and that there were very few people she would call that. I still remain baffled by this feeling of hers. I like her, find her, although very reserved, warmer than most English

people, and admire greatly her poem *The Land*.
But I couldn't remotely think of her as a friend.
Indeed, I don't even feel as though I know or
understand her. She is obviously a very deep and
complex person. I suppose she likes me because I
am direct and outgoing and practically a peasant
in contrast to her formidable Sackville inheritance.

2

May 20 Aboard S.S. *Queen Elizabeth*. It has taken me
two days to recuperate from the exhaustion that
gradually overcame me in London. I saw many
friends, was never alone at all. But apparently my
Proust-focused mind was still in Paris, and non-
Proustian encounters, no matter how warm and
friendly, slid over me too dreamily to have any impact, except admiration for the gallantry and courage with which Londoners face rebuilding their
city and their lives. Things are better than they
were two months ago when the snow-dotted ruins
made me weep. The lifts in the hotel are running.
With the longer days the limitations on lighting
are less troublesome. And as always in the spring,
there are windowboxes full of hydrangeas in front
of many shops. The very presence of these cultivated blooms was partly responsible for the shock
I experienced as I window-shopped slowly down
Bond Street. Suddenly at the corner of Conduit
Street there were no shops, no windows to look in,
just the largest gaping bomb-hole I had seen. If it
had just been rubble-filled or barren it would
merely have saddened me. But from that huge hole

EL PROUST AT THE AGE
ENTY. Jacques-Émile
he, a fellow-visitor at Les
onts, Mme. Laure
ères' Trouville villa,
this sketch in October
or his better-known
fied portrait of Proust
at the Salon des Artistes
ais in 1892.
S.P.A.D.E.M. Paris, 1978.

MARCEL PROUST A 21 ANS
(Trouville, les Frémonts, 29 Août 1892)

Dessin inédit de Paul Baignères
retrouvé dans un album du temps.

PROUST IN A DRAWING BY PAUL
BAIGNÈRES, Mme. Baignères' son. It
was made in August 1892 when
Proust and his childhood friend,
Louis de La Salle, were staying at
Les Frémonts.

MADAME MARIE SCHEIKÉVITCH. More of a blue-stocking than most fashionable hostesses of the period, she first met Proust in 1912, a year before *Swann's Way* appeared, and made efforts to help with the book's publication.

THE DUCHESSE DE CLERMONT-TONNER in a portrait by Laszlo, painted at the tu of the century when her long friendship with Proust began.

GENEVIÈVE HALÉVY BIZET STRAUS, circa Mme. Straus was the daughter of Frome: Halévy, composer of the opera *La Juive*; widow of Georges Bizet, composer of *Carmen*; and wife of Emile Straus, a wea lawyer connected with the Rothschilds. I salon, the short-lived magazine *Le Banq* was launched by her son Jacques Bizet, N Proust, and several of their schoolmates.

THE AUTHOR IN 1955,
shortly before the
publication of *Bizet
and his World*.

(Left) MADAME CÉLESTE ALBARET in 19
Proust's housekeeper, nurse and guardia
angel from 1913 until his death in 1922.

(Top Right) CÉLESTE AND ODILON ALBA
at the wedding of their daughter in 1955.
Odilon was the driver of the taxi which w
Proust's disposal night and day.

(Bottom Left) THE HÔTEL D'ALSACE ET
LORRAINE in the rue des Cannettes, whic
Céleste and Odilon Albaret owned and ra
many years.

(Bottom Right) CÉLESTE'S HOUSE AT MÉ
near Montfort-l'Amaury, where she has
since her husband's death.

INCE ANTOINE BIBESCO.
manian diplomat and
nch playwright, he was a
se and immensely helpful
end to Proust for twenty
rs.

QUAI DE BOURBON, Prince
ntoine's residence on the
St.-Louis, at the prow of
e island.

A LETTER FROM PROUST TO BIBESCO, which the prince gave me and later published, omitting the portions he crossed out.

AN ENVELOPE ADDRESSED TO PROUST BY BIBESCO, on the back of which Proust scribbled a message to Céleste about ordering medicine: ''This box of Voger [?] granules seems to me to be empty. I find neither the Ranni [?] syrup nor the Gorneol [?].''

S 1890s PHOTOGRAPH OF
?UST with the Marquis de
?rs *(left),* future popular
?ywright, and Lucien Daudet
?ht), son of Alphonse,
?ressed Proust's mother.

?low Left) THE COMTESSE
?FFULHE, in a portrait by
?est Hébert. Proust wrote that
?ll the mystery of her beauty is
?he brilliance, the enigma of
?eyes. I have never seen such a
?utiful woman . . . . ''

?low Right) THE ABBÉ
?GNIER, PAINTED BY THE
?MTESSE GREFFULHE.
?harming cultivated man,
?cribed as ''an apostle to the
?bourg St.-Germain,'' he
?tinually dined out in
?nionable society while living in
?utmost poverty. Proust was
?oted to him and told Céleste
?'Send for the good Abbé
?gnier half an hour after I die.
?u will see how he'll pray for
?''

THE COMTE ROBERT DE MONTESQUI
Proust's mentor as a young man and
his chief model for the Baron Charlu
He was the Comtesse Greffulhe's
cousin, and is shown holding the
chinchilla cape she lent to him when l
wanted something of hers included ir
this portrait by Whistler.

DANIEL HALÉVY IN HIS EIGHTIES—
schoolmate of Proust and distinguishe
historian who generously helped me in
research on Proust and Bizet.

in the middle of the city sprang great masses of wild pink fire-weed. Here nature, so often a gardener's enemy, had with flamboyant generosity covered the ugliness wrought by human beings. The sight of those brilliant flower spikes became for me, illogically enough, a symbol of British indomitability.

The only other time I remember seeing fire-weed goes back over forty years when I was at a girls' camp in a wild part of Canada. Thick green forests surrounded the lake shore along which most of the trails were cut. But once, portaging a canoe from one lake to another, we came upon acres of stark, black tree stumps. Only the dense ground cover of irrepressible fire-weed softened the impact of that shocking, almost murderous sight. It was the kind of experience one would think unforgettable. Yet it remained buried in my mind until that morning in London when the sight of nature's benign covering of the crime deliberately committed by human beings upon other human beings evoked the image of those charred, black trunks of once-living trees, destroyed, unintentionally no doubt, by human beings.

Until now I have been too weary to do more than glance at the passenger list. However, the stewardess informed me that there are many celebrities on board, including Michael Arlen, Noel Coward, and Bea Lillie. Today when I went down the list I discovered that Rebecca West is a fellow passenger. The unexpected sight of her name on the passenger list served as a *madeleine* reminding me of her first visit to Harry and me in Northampton in 1926, the year we were married.

I wanted Rebecca to see the charm of the Connecticut valley landscape and as I have always preferred spicing scenic expeditions with some sort of human focus we drove to Avon where Mrs. Theodate Pope Riddle, a pioneer woman architect, was building a much-discussed boys' school.

The impact of our meeting I shall never forget. Her appearance itself was memorable. Mrs. Riddle was rather tall, and large-bosomed in a pouter-pigeonish sort of way. Her costume seemed to symbolize an inner conflict between the male and female aspects of her nature, a conflict of which I am sure she was unaware. She was clad in some sort of brown leather knickerbockers, and above these rather bloomerlike pants she wore a very delicate made-in-France looking blouse with val lace inserted in narrow strips. On her commanding bosom a sky blue enamel watch hung from a jeweled butterfly pin.

Mrs. Riddle immediately set about showing us her amazing creation which spread over many acres. The style of the school itself was pure Tudor — stone and wood, every inch cut and hewn by hand. The building resembled poor-house cottages in a well-preserved Elizabethan village — low-roofed with leaded windows too small to permit enough daylight to read by.

In contrast to these low buildings there rose behind them a very high-seeming water tower about double the size of a silo and built of handsome bricks, variegated in size and color. Its noticeably sagging contours were explained by Mrs. Riddle's prejudice against such mechanical devices as a plumb line. She admitted that the tower had necessarily been rebuilt several times.

Even more striking than the tower squatted a building in such architectural contrast to the others that one could only gasp. Undersized, but still lording it over its Tudor neighbors, stood a Greek Revival structure rendered, columns and all, in native Connecticut red stone. It seemed a parody of the many banks built in the nineteenth century throughout New England. Although it bore no identification as yet, I risked asking whether it was a bank. It was indeed. Either Rebecca or I asked Mrs. Riddle how she happened to choose that particular style for it.

"It came to me in my sleep," she said. "I always think about a plan when I go to bed. Then during the night a plan comes to me and in the morning I can draft it just as it should be."

"Don't you ever have to change anything?" Rebecca asked. "No blocks! No blank pages you gaze at for hours and days! Everything always right the first time!"

"Oh, yes," said Mrs. Riddle, "I never have any trouble."

Afterthought, 1977

When re-reading my account of this adventure I fortunately found in my file a letter of Rebecca's far livelier than my largely visual recollection. Here it is:

. . . Mrs. Riddle when unmarried went to London with a young man to a spiritualist conference and chose the *Lusitania* as vessel. She went right down and came up! The young man was drowned . . . She is always adopting children and finding out that they are unsuitable two or three years later. All this I had from Mrs. Whitelaw Reid who told me this with many a snort. She has been all over the school and says it is all very dark, just

like the rooms we saw. "Slum conditions, slum conditions!" she snorted. I was so ravished by the idea of the
pigskin breeches going down to the Atlantic bottom that
I felt like telegraphing you . . .

I have opened this letter to inform you that last night
I met a man who listened while I was talking about the
cottages and said in a puzzled way, "I can't understand
that school. She doesn't seem to have engaged a staff but
she has bought my mother's prize bull." This, in view of
her terse declaration of her curriculum, I think wonderful.

Another day On my first tour around the deck I spotted Rebecca, ensconced in a corner steamer chair by herself. She asked me to sit down in the chair next to
her and tell her what I had been doing. So I told
her about my work and that I had been in Paris
meeting Proust's friends. A light kindled in her
eyes and she asked whether I had met Antoine
Bibesco. "Not you, too, Rebecca," I said, and then
we both laughed, reunited through Antoine's penchant for bluestockings, so differently expressed
from Clive's.

A night or two later Rebecca dined with me and
we had a rather extraordinary conversation about
something which until that moment I had quite
forgotten. In 1915 or 1916, when I was an undergraduate and she was in her early twenties, she
published a series of essays in *The New Republic*
called "Woman: The World's Worst Failure."
The theme was women's freedom. The subject of
each essay focused on a woman of a different class
or type, each of whom was trapped either by the
social conditions that surrounded her or by the
flaws in her own character.

"I think that was when I first decided that freedom was the most important thing in a woman's
life," I said. "But now that I really am totally free,
I'm not sure I haven't paid too high a price for it."

Rebecca hesitated for a moment and then said,
"I've never had a free moment in my life."

Suddenly the image of Dr. Anna Howard Shaw,
of Mrs. Carrie Chapman Catt and the other ladies
at the National Woman's Suffrage Association
came back to me. When I was a boarder at their
headquarters in Washington during my M.I.5 days
in 1918, they found my inactivity in the movement
deplorable, my reasoning contemptible. I merely
said that I knew women would get the vote as they
should, but that I was equally sure they would use
it the same way men always had. They would have
to change a great deal before achieving the kind of
freedom these good ladies envisaged. My kind of
freedom, and Rebecca's — for of course her con-
tention was an example of her penchant for occasional dramatic hyperbole — would have shocked
them very much.

How far from Proust I have strayed! Little anxiety about freedom for women other than sexual
disturbed the author of *La Prisonnière* and *Albertine disparue*.

PART
THREE

Chapter 9

THE TOIL AND TROUBLE of the periods between my 1947 and my two 1948 visits to Paris are brought back to me only by the letters in my file. I had quite forgotten those particular publishers' blues. They have been succeeded by many others.

For a brief summary of the conditions under which I improved the translation, wrote the notes, made the index, and read the proof of *Letters of Marcel Proust* I have recourse to my correspondence.

"This project has in some ways been a headache for both of us," wrote my editor, Bob Linscott, in accepting the typescript in September 1948. "But when we look back at it from the vantage point of years, I have a hunch that this may be the episode of our lives of which we can both be proudest — you for the work and me for persuading you to undertake it. For the letters and (I hope) the biography to follow are bound to give you an international reputation and a kind of literary immortality."

To which combination of under- and overstatement I replied: "What you say about the book having been a headache is indeed true. For me it has also been a heartache and a stomach ache. However, soon all these complications will be in the past, and I fortunately have a well-developed gift for forgetting unpleasant episodes. As far as my reputation goes I don't see how I can have much of one except as a translator until after the other book is finished."

Before telling the nature of the disagreements it is only fair to say that I was granted a year's postponement of the deadline. But there was no compromise about the changes in editing to include the information I had collected in Paris. My contract said that the paragraphs identifying Proust's correspondents should be as brief as possible. However, I felt, and still feel, that character portraits of the most important correspondents, forming a sort of link between the letters, would have made the book much livelier and more interesting. Denied this wish, I promptly decided to write a biography of Proust, a project soon superseded by the life of a quite different sort of artist.

Another conflict, causing additional tension, concerned the index. I am admittedly fanatical about indexes. Before reading any biography I always first examine the index. So my rage knew no bounds when I discovered that without consulting me a young man had been hired to make mine. After receiving his version I wrote to Bob: "The mistakes in the index are like a rolling snowball. Not only are there serious omissions, but mistakes in pagination, spelling, and in the identification of names. For instance the Duc de Saint-Simon is listed as Comte de, thereby transforming Louis XIV's memorialist into the late eighteenth and early nineteenth century philosopher. Also who would guess that 'George, David L.' was Lloyd-George?"

I still remember resentfully the days and nights spent checking that index, a kind of specialized work for which I am ill equipped and fortunately have never had to do again. My bitterness, however, was eventually sweetened by a letter from Antoine, whom I asked to examine the published index in the hope that there might be an edition in the original French. (There wasn't.)

"*Chèrie,*" he wrote, "I am dazzled by your index. I put off reading it from day to day thinking it would be an immense job. So I was delighted to find it very easy. There were only three small mistakes . . . Your book is brilliant and I congratulate you."

This cooperation although flattering was, alas, much too late to be helpful. During the year between my first two visits to Paris when I was struggling to finish a collection which would have been quite incomplete without his letters from Proust, Antoine's behavior was wholly erratic. For the first few weeks after I came home to Ashfield there arrived a spate of brief notes, scrawls he called love letters, adolescent bits of eroticism which I promptly destroyed. Then several months of silence, followed by a letter explaining that he had been in Rumania where all of his property and holdings had been confiscated by the Communist government. After his return, forced to face the fact that he was really a poor man, in spite of some funds in Switzerland, he wrote almost daily letters.

The first one included a photocopy of the inscription in a presentation copy of *Les Plaisirs et les jours*. It read: "*A Antoine Bibesco qui j'aime et qui j'admire, 30 octobre, 1901, six heures du soir. Bonne nuit aimable Prince et que des essaims d'anges bercent en chantant vôtre sommeil. Marcel Proust.*"

Along with this unusable document Antoine enclosed the following holograph letter from Proust, large parts of which were heavily blacked out, some in India, some in red ink. "I have suppressed only purely personal passages in the letter," he wrote. "These autographs I am sending you are not a substitute for the one or two letters of Marcel Proust that I promised to send you."

> My dear Antoine,
> There is one point at least about which I can tell you
> . . . to promise me not to make an inquiry and not to

violate *Tombeau*. It is this about which I should have
... talked in person. Among other things that you actually said there is this. You told several persons who
don't know each other that . . .

I give you this sad warning so that you understand
why, in the true sense of the word I am no longer your
friend. And what astonishes me is that the satisfaction
(wholly negative however without any exhilaration) of
not seeing you when I don't see you, can suddenly be
followed by the *very great* delight when I do see you as
I did this evening.

The fact is that your self, your very physical entity,
still holds the unconscious memory of the marvelous
qualities you had, but which have been materialized,
changed by your self-destructive evil genius, into nothing
more than a way of looking, inflections of a voice, a gesture which, nevertheless, retain for a person who has
known them the charm of a particularly touching image,
such as objects leave of themselves, create of themselves
an imprint which will have meaning and beauty.

From another point of view, since sympathy is at the
root of my nature, I would rather recreate within myself
the states of mind that bring me close to others than
those that separate me from them *forever and ever*.

So the memory of the rare kindnesses you have done
me (I don't mean that there weren't many, but on the
contrary, that they were of a rare and exquisite kind)
often return to make me wish not to remind myself of a
person from whom so many ineffaceable injuries have
estranged me but to do him good if I were given the opportunity, which, alas, given my situation in life would
appear to be very unlikely. But this in itself is the reason
it might be possible. So if ever under given circumstances I can be temporarily useful to you I should be

happy to have you remember that in that exceptional and specific way I remain your devoted and grateful
                                                    Marcel Proust
I should be very happy if M. Vuillard would consent to sell me the sketch of the dinner at Armenonville last year — a case of unique coincidence between his admirable talent which often enriches my memory of one charming and perfect hour of my life. You would be doing me a favor to ask him.

The flattering portion of this letter Antoine included in his edition of Proust's letters without mentioning his bowdlerization. With a great deal of eyestrain, labor, and assistance from experts I was able to decipher most of the deleted portions of the letter, but not the ones that revealed the exact nature of Antoine's offense. The key, however, is *"tombeau,"* the word that symbolized an agreement between the friends the nature of which Antoine described in an excerpt from his unpublished memoirs:

At twenty when I was a devoted reader of detective stories I believed that friendship could be secret and absolute. Marcel Proust seemed so confiding that one day I proposed to him a pact by which I would keep him informed of other people's opinion of him and he would tell me what they said about me without anyone's knowing.

For instance I told him that Porto-Riche [a successful playwright] had advised me not to associate with him because it would give me a bad reputation.

I also told him that Léon Daudet [reactionary journalist responsible for Proust's being awarded the Prix Goncourt] whom I saw at my cousin's, Anna de Noailles [noted poet in her day], stated that Proust's poor health was due to morphine (which was not true).

Marcel, however, did not play the game and never told me any indiscretions. The pact I dreamed up was broken in spite of which I found Marcel Proust an incomparable friend.

This rather elliptical explanation hardly clarifies the letter Antoine sent me. But Antoine's breach of confidence, which was surely not unique, only briefly interrupted their friendship.

Useless as this letter was for my purposes, I must have thanked him for it suitably. For in his next letter he wrote:

> Darling, (1) A million thanks for your letter. (2) Could you arrange a lecture tour for me on Proust or European politics? (3) I hoped your brother was rich and would invite me to America by plane. (4) Please send me some jam and nylon stockings (size 9) for my daughter. I am sending you $20. (5) Suppose I wanted to sell 200 original letters of Marcel Proust would I find a buyer in America? (6) Give me Céleste's address. (7) Having found you I don't mean to lose you anymore. *Je t'embrasse partout.* A.

I quickly offered to sell the letters for him — a perfect chance for me to read them all and choose the ones I wanted to publish. On October 8, 1947, he wrote, "I am entrusting you with the sale of my Marcel Proust letters. First I will have them photocopied, and then I will send them to you." He never sent the copies, but in the nick of time I did eventually see the letters.

The problem of pinning Antoine down to a date when I could examine them was in a sense only a minor anxiety that summer. For, after all, I did know where they were and that it would be to his eventual advantage to let me see them. Far more troubling was the problem of discovering the originals of Marcel's letters to Mme. Straus. There seemed to be no clue to the whereabouts of the mysterious Mme. Sibilat who owned them. And since I had chosen more letters to Mme. Straus than to any other correspondent, it was immensely important to insure the correctness of the text. After collating the published version of her letters with the excerpts from the proof that M. Halévy had given me, I could see that the original transcriptions were obviously faulty. So I was determined to compare at least the letters I had translated with their originals.

2

Today, as I re-read my choice of Proust's letters to Mme. Straus I am inclined to think it was based on subjective rather than sound editorial judgment. For there is no doubt that at that time I did identify with Geneviève Bizet Straus. Her having been widowed young, as I had been, after her brief but happy marriage to Bizet, naturally gave rise to my feeling of sympathy. In a flattering portrait of her wearing widow's weeds I thought I could discern a certain resemblance between us. But most of all I envied her the privilege of watching Marcel, her son Jacques Bizet's brilliant schoolmate, develop from a talented but perhaps precious, shallow writer into the great genius he became. On another level I envied her as the Egeria of a salon frequented by so many of the distinguished writers and artists of her day.

Envy is a feckless emotion, and my particular variation of it was singularly silly. Indeed, not until I was sixty or more did I cease sporadically nursing the notion that I would like to have a salon. I knew as many distinguished artists as she did, though they were not often on the same side of the Atlantic. However, having so rarely been a guest at any salons myself, it took me rather a long time to realize that to attract the necessary talented and gifted habitués more is required than a preferably rich, reasonably engaging, intelligent hostess. In addition to the lions there must also be sycophants in the form of society people, as well as disciples and protégés of the celebrities, flatterers to listen and to mollify the tension so often created by articulately competitive fellow artists. Fortunately my aversion to small talk, my inability to suffer fools gladly precluded my ever trying to carry out in life the fantasy engendered by my first image of Mme. Straus. Proust's early characterization of her which I originally chose to ignore, attributing it to youthful jealousy, now seems to me the most accurate portrayal.

"The Truth about Madame Straus" he headed a letter written when he was twenty: "At first I believed you loved only beautiful things and that you understood them very well — and then I saw that you didn't give a hang about them; then I thought you liked people, and now I see you don't give a hang about them either. I believe you love only a certain kind of life which brings out your intelligence less than your wit, your wit less than your tact, your tact less than your clothes. A person who more than anything loves this kind of life — and who, nevertheless, casts a spell!"

However, it was her remark after Bizet's death, quoted by Gounod, that moved me most: "There is not an hour, not a minute of the six years of happiness which my married life brought me that I would not gladly live over again." The fact that Gounod as a close family friend invented and circulated this statement in order to scotch the rumor that Geneviève was partly responsible for Bizet's early death I discovered only some time later. Then my search for Proust's letters to her had led me to her unpublished family letters, a discovery that seduced me into becoming a professional biographer.

Chapter 10

O N APRIL FOOLS' DAY, 1948, I returned to Paris. That evening Antoine dined with me and after giving me an affectionate bear hug asked me to marry him. To the only honorable proposal I had received in nineteen years of widowhood my response was not predictable. I burst into roars of laughter and said, "Darling, whatever gave you such an idea?" It was his daughter, he said.

"Priscilla thinks that if I married you, you would take good care of me."

"She's quite right," I agreed. "If I married you I would take very good care of you."

As I spoke there flashed through my mind the picture of my remote house in the Berkshire foothills, the reactions of my Scotch housekeeper and Yankee gardener, subjected to feudal princely behavior. "It might work out," I said, "if we didn't first murder each other by mistake." Rather like the gingham dog and the calico cat, I thought. "And do you think a Jewish Rumanian princess would be suitable?" I asked. That aspect had not occurred to him. Indeed he never showed any signs of anti-Semitism.

"You tell Priscilla that you followed her excellent advice. But being in my own way as much a monster as you are, I don't think a marriage would work."

Antoine seemed greatly relieved, and from that time on we had an *amitié amoureuse* the memory of which I cherish. Why this is true, the reader, basing his impressions on the account of Antoine's behavior in my diary, may well wonder. And as I re-read it now I can see that my professional determination to see Proust's letters caused me to emphasize the obstacles in my way rather than the attraction of the man who raised them.

During my second stay in Paris I ceased keeping a diary because I had the good fortune to meet on shipboard Liliane Yacoël, now Mme. Olivier Ziegel, a most remarkable young Frenchwoman who became my research assistant. Her gift for all aspects of research, her accuracy in reporting interviews precluded any need of my resuming journal-keeping. So to give a fair picture of a period that now, after more than a quarter of a century, seems rather like a fantasy that happened to somebody else, I am dependent for *aides-mémoires* not on other people's letters but on my own.

To a very old friend, John Houseman, who from a director and producer has now in his seventies become an Oscar-winning film star, I wrote:

> What is there about you fantastic, theatre-struck, unreliable French Rumanians that I find so cozy? I assure you that if Antoine were ten years younger (thank God he isn't. Me as a *Princesse* would be pretty funny) my glib turning down last night of the first honorable proposal I've had since Harry died would have been more difficult. He says his daughter wishes him to marry me and I think she's a very wise daughter indeed. I would certainly look after him nicely because he enchants me. For a man who must have lied fairly consistently for

nearly twenty years (by profession he used to be a diplomat) he does it with such admirably transparent
charm ... He has aged a good deal in the last year. For
half an hour I extracted splendid Proustian lore from
him. But his mind is a disorderly gold mine and his
memory is incredibly capricious. In any case I feel surprisingly at home with him, partly due to the long train-
ing from you summed up in your often repeated remark,
"That, darling, is not the sort of thing you can count on
me for" ... He's taking me to the opening of the new
Sartre play tomorrow. I'll write you about it ... I think
I'll spend next winter here if there isn't a war and nobody
thinks there will be that soon. Why I feel so wonderfully
at home in this city I know so little I can't tell except
that I adore being made a fuss over and having my room
filled with flowers and *hommage,* etc. So many telephone calls! So many invitations!

My use of the word "cozy" seems oddly inappropriate in today's
perspective, but a letter to my mother explains the reason:

Antoine lectures me and worries about how much money
I spend, hiring a car for all of a dollar an hour when
there are no taxis available, etc. Finally I simply said to
him, "When you were rich did you worry about spending money all the time?" He admitted he didn't. So I
assured him that if I were going to be poor one day I
could take it just as well as he does (which I must say is
really very well, indeed). Only would he please stop trying to make me economize so that he won't feel embarrassed at not being able to entertain me in the manner to
which we are accustomed. Each time someone sends me
a larger plant than he did he has a fit, and he just called
up to suggest that instead of going to a theatre tomorrow

night for which he would need a car that we should go to one within walking distance. I pointed out that the play was what interested me. I think he has now decided on Folies-Bergère and I don't really care because he amuses me so much.

He says I remind him of Margot Asquith — mother of Antoine's wife who died three years ago. Naturally I am flattered. One day he showed me something she said about him in her memoirs: "Antoine Bibesco is remarkable both as talker and listener. Had my son-in-law been compelled to earn his living he has enough brains and ability to have made fame and fortune in any walk of life. He is handsome and kind and my relation to him is not that which is usually connected with mothers-in-law." He is one of the few men I know who both likes clever women and is easy to be with. That's what I really like best about him. When he behaves *en Prince* I have told him I can't bear it. So he is now not only civil to waiters but quite considerate of me. For a man of seventy he is incredibly energetic and young looking, but he has aged a good deal since last year.

As for Proust's letters, I did eventually see them in time to choose and translate some before my deadline. They were eventually sold through the efforts of my friend Professor Philip Kolb, long-time authority on the dating of Proust's letters and now editor of the new edition of Proust's *Correspondance Générale*. Neither Philip nor I can remember clearly the chronology of the delays, the intrigue, the procrastination inevitable in any dealings with Antoine. But I do know that at some point I brought back to the United States a huge album of Proust's letters, apparently the one I had briefly held on my lap the first day I visited the Quai de Bourbon. I still have a concrete visual image of the stormy Atlantic crossing when that precious album slid back and

forth from under my berth with every roll of the heavy sea —
the letters destined to find their resting place at the University
of Illinois in Urbana.

2

The word "cozy," as I have said, rings oddly in my ears today
in relation to Antoine. "Relaxed" would I think have been more
accurate. Cozy applies far more to my familylike relation with
the Albarets. If I didn't take at least one meal a week at Céleste's
her feelings would be hurt, so I ate dinner there nearly every
Sunday in the spring of 1948. And wonderful dinners they
were — food and talk both on a gourmet level.

We would sit from one o'clock to five or six in those stiff-
backed chairs, eating hors d'oeuvres, chicken — ("But Madame,
you don't like *mon petit poulet*. You're not taking another help-
ing. Céleste is a poor cook, you think?") — followed by braised
endive and *une petite salade de laitue,* a magnificent tart, and
cheese and fruit. And as Odilon opened bottle after bottle of
wine to warm us, Proust's name would come into the conversation
as naturally as that of some beloved member of the family, absent
on a journey. More often than not the violent arguments between Céleste and Odilon would be settled by the introduction
of some remark which the master must have employed many
times to settle the very same argument. Always Proust seemed
to be there, hovering somewhere, unseen, smiling ironically, but
without surprise, that here alone, in this grim and dreary room,
he, the supposedly great snob writer, should be kept alive by the
warmth and love of the people who had known and served him
best. Sometimes Céleste would say, "Madame, when you are
here it seems as though M. Proust himself came back," and for
me he did. For in her casual, spontaneous conversation she revealed so many different sides of both the man and the writer.

Céleste started working for Proust in 1913 when her chief function was delivering copies of the first edition of *Swann* to his friends. Not until Odilon went to war in 1914 did she actually live in the apartment. "I naturally started to go to Mass the first Sunday morning," Céleste told me. "When Monsieur saw me with my hat and coat on he said, 'But where are you going, Céleste? You wouldn't go out and leave me here alone, would you?' When I explained that I was going to Mass he looked at me sadly and said, 'My good Céleste, surely *le bon Dieu* is as likely to grant you your place in heaven for nursing a poor sick man as for leaving him to go to Mass.' So, Madame, I never went to Mass again while Monsieur was alive. Sometimes I used to feel like a captive, a prisoner, never going out except on errands for him. And sometimes I would think of leaving because when he was irritable he was very difficult. He would avoid seeing me and then I would cry. But always, Madame, he made up for it. He would be so gay and delightful that Odilon and I would laugh for hours when he imitated the people he met at parties. Sometimes he would talk about them. 'Tonight was a successful evening,' he would smile and say. 'I must go to work at once. I heard something perfect for Mme. Verdurin to say.' Always, Madame, you see, he was thinking about his work" . . . "No, Madame, no matter how difficult it was, how imprisoned I sometimes felt in that strange house, I was attached to him by the very peculiarities of his nature. I could not leave M. Proust. He was so good."

Proust's virtue, or the state of his soul, was a source of anxiety to at least one of his friends, the Abbé Mugnier who, Jacques-Emile Blanche has said, "was one of the richest, most stimulating of Proust's sources of social information. . . . When the Abbé Mugnier tried to recall him to the duties of the spirit, Proust replied, 'I would rather hear you talk about Comte Aimery de la Rochefoucauld.' " The Abbé Mugnier, for many years the favorite priest of the Faubourg, was responsible for the conversion of

Huysmans. But later, because of his *mondanité,* he was deprived of his parish and appointed confessor to a convent of nuns. Once when he was leaving after a visit to Proust, Céleste heard him say, *"Il faut que j'aille confesser mes poules mystiques."* Another time when Proust asked him his opinion of *Les fleurs du mal,* he replied, pointing to his heart, *"Elles sont toujours ici avec moi."*

Perhaps Proust regarded his friendship with the Abbé as a sort of hostage against his entry into a possible next world, for when he was dying he told Céleste to send for the Abbé to pray for his soul, but in no circumstances to notify him until fifteen minutes after his death. Death was, naturally enough, a subject with which Proust was frequently preoccupied. And Céleste thought that he approached it in the same scientific spirit he brought to all subject matter necessary to his novel.

"M. Proust had to know everything," she said one day in the course of a conversation. (And I shall give here the exact notes I wrote down immediately afterward.) "He even had to know what death was like. I am sure that is what happened when once in 1918 he didn't ring for nearly two days . . . One could never disturb him. That was forbidden. His mother would have turned in her grave at a servant's coming into his room unless he rang. This time I stayed and talked to him until about three in the morning and then I went to bed. I waited from eight o'clock on for him to ring but he didn't, not all that day or that night. The next morning I went quietly, quietly, on tiptoe to listen at the door and not a sound could I hear. Then I went downstairs to the apartment below to talk to a lady, a chambermaid, and she thought I ought to go in, but I was afraid to. Then at last, at two o'clock, he rang. I went in and said, 'Ah, Monsieur, I was so worried about you.'

" 'You had reason to be, Céleste,' he answered and then motioned to me the way he used to, not to speak or ask anything. 'I'll tell you later,' he said. Later he asked me what I had been worried about and I told him that I was afraid I might never see

him again. 'You don't know how close you came to it,' he said
... I think, Madame, that he took the largest possible dose of
veronal he dared take and still be sure of going on living while
feeling and knowing what death was like ... Isn't there somewhere in *Swann* — of course, I haven't read it so I don't know —
but isn't there a passage that describes such an experience?"

Often there were other visitors. Sometimes it was Céleste's
sister, Marie Gineste, a small white-haired spinster with an engaging habit of nodding a little at table in a sort of sociable
slumber, out of which she would wake suddenly and enter into
the conversation as though she had been participating the whole
time. Proust wrote of her, "Marie Gineste was more regularly
rapid and abrupt, Céleste Albaret softer and more languishing,
spread out like a lake, but with terrible boiling rages in which her
fury suggested the peril of spates and gales that sweep everything
before them."

Sometimes it was Odilon's sister who came — a bright, cheerful little old lady in spite of her devouring religiosity. (From
devout Protestantism she had been converted late in life to
equally devout Catholicism.) She brought to show me one day
four worn, cherished sheets of writing paper, the extraordinarily
personal, deeply sympathetic letter Marcel Proust had written
her when her only daughter died in childbirth. Relatives from
the provinces or the colonies, cousins from Toulouse or Algiers
would turn up sometimes too. Always their manners were perfect,
their questions about America astute in contrast to the clichés
addressed to me by "the Verdurins."

3

Until 1947, the twenty-fifth anniversary of Proust's death,
Céleste led a wholly secluded life, working long days, scrubbing
and cleaning the little workingmen's hotel, acting as gracious

hostess to her humble guests. (Occasionally scandalmongers had sought her out, offered her large sums of money for scurrilous information about her master's life. The cold dignity with which they were dismissed is easily pictured.) In late 1947, however, the Bibliothèque Nationale held a Proust exhibition in honor of the anniversary. Among the exhibits were the manuscripts of the last three volumes of the novel, loaned by Mme. Mante. In these manuscripts, Julien Cain, the director of the library, noticed some handwriting that was obviously not Proust's. Having heard about Céleste, he managed with considerable difficulty to discover her address and to invite her to come to the exhibit. She was full of the adventure when I returned to Paris. M. Cain himself had been gracious enough to escort her around the exhibition rooms. "And as I was leaving, Madame, M. le Directeur asked me for my autograph because, he said, it would be an honor and a pleasure for him to have it. So I took off my glove and I wrote, not just my signature, Madame, but a long autograph, as long as a *dédicace* of M. Proust's ... For I understood and appreciated M. Cain's tact and courtesy. But, Madame, I need not tell you that I knew M. Cain wanted to compare my handwriting with the writing in the manuscript to make sure whose it was. Now there can be no mistake, even if sometimes I do write the same letter two or three different ways on the same page."

After this official recognition, Celeste received an increasing number of literary visitors. She was interviewed on the Paris radio and a "cocktail" was given in her honor at the radio station. This function, she then told me, she was reluctant to attend, for it did not seem to her suitable or correct for a woman in her humble circumstances to be lionized because of her connection with M. Proust. Of Proust's feeling for her she naturally divulged nothing in public. But I remember her saying to me one day, "At heart, M. Proust distrusted everyone. He didn't really trust even me until he was dying — and I couldn't believe he was dying . . . I was so young, Madame. My world centered around him. I couldn't believe my world could stop so soon — only when he was dying did he start really trusting me. 'Céleste,' he would say, 'you have nursed me as though you were my mother. Had I been your child you couldn't have tended me with more care. Why, Céleste, why are you so good to me?' . . . Madame, I was only thirty-two. Everything I knew about life Monsieur had taught me. I couldn't believe he was dying . . . 'I must leave you something in my will,' he said. 'Do you think if I made a new will now, Céleste, it would stand, or would they say I was too ill to know what I was doing?' 'But, Monsieur, you mustn't think that way,' I said. 'You are not going to die. You can't die' . . . Madame, I did not know then what I know today . . . But he warned me. He predicted everything. He always knew what would happen. 'At first, Céleste,' he said, 'all my friends will come to see you. They will want to help you. Out of affection for my memory they will make you offers you will be too proud to accept. But gradually they will forget. And after a year or two only X and Y and perhaps Z will come to see you.' " I asked her who among the friends had continued to see her. She rather shunned answering the question, and as far as I could make out Mme. Scheikévitch was the only one. About an episode involving Dr. Robert Proust, Marcel's brother, and Reynaldo Hahn, who had called every day during his old friend's last illness without ever seeing him, Céleste gave me an account more suggestive of Balzac's *La Cousine Bette* than Swann's or the Guermantes' way.

"Monsieur had given me a copy of the rare edition of *Jeunes Filles en fleur* with a piece of the manuscript in it. He said that after he died I could sell it for three thousands francs and that years later it would be worth twelve thousand. The book was on the table next to his bed when he died and later Dr. Proust picked it up and started to take it with him. But I told him that it was my copy that his brother had given me in case I was ever in need. He then said of course he wouldn't take it but I said that I was only a simple woman who couldn't read the works of M. Proust, that I would never sell it but that I would like to give it to M. Reynaldo Hahn who was a great friend of Proust's. So Dr. Proust took it and said he would give it to Hahn. I never heard from M. Hahn so I wrote to him after a long time to ask whether he had ever received it. He wrote back that Dr. Proust had never told him it was a present from me."

When I left Céleste's one Sunday in late April 1948 for an appointment at the Hôtel Plaza-Athénée, it would have been quite impossible to foresee the changing course of our future destinies, though mine was certainly more predictable than hers.

Chapter 11

O<small>N</small> A<small>PRIL</small> 24 I wrote my mother:

The most really incredible thing has happened to me — the one thing in the world, except to get at Proust's *cahiers,* that I wanted to have happen. I actually have here in my room at the hotel a dozen or more morocco-bound albums of letters and manuscripts that belonged to Mme. Straus. Here is how it came about. I knew last year that Proust's letters to Mme. Straus had been in the possession of M. Straus' heir, his nephew René Sibilat. But I knew nothing about him except that he was supposed to have given them to the Bibliothèque Nationale twenty years ago and hadn't. So I asked M. Halévy about it the first time I met him and he told me that Sibilat had died recently leaving everything to his widow. Many years ago after Straus' death M. Halévy had brought a lawsuit against Sibilat to try to get him to give these things to the Nationale. But M. Halévy lost the suit. He could tell me nothing about the whereabouts of Sibilat's widow and it has taken me all this time to find her.

I then proceeded to ask everyone I met whether they knew a Mme. Sibilat. At first nobody did. But in less than a week at a stupid cocktail party I met a rather unattractive man who turned out to have been her *homme d'affaires* until yesterday, when she fired him. He did not feel kindly toward her. She is mad as a hatter, he said, Danish, fabulously rich and wholly under the influence of an American Dr. Bayon who happens to have been my doctor when I had sinus last year. So I wrote him a note, reminding him of me and my work about which I had told him a little, and said I would be very grateful if he could arrange for me to see her and to look at the letters. For several days I had no reply but when I came in at midnight on Saturday from dinner at the Yacoëls' I found a message saying that Mme. Sibilat would receive me at the Plaza-Athénée the following day between five and seven.

It was an unbelievable day, warm and sunny and all the chestnut trees starting to bloom. I spent from one to five at Céleste's in her windowless combination dining, sitting and bed-room and came away with the loan of a copy of *Chartreuse de Parme* that Proust had annotated. I then went into the sunny splendor of the Athénée and found that Mme. S. was out. I sat for nearly an hour in the lobby glancing at Proust's notes in the *Chartreuse*, watching each person who came in, picturing her as an old lady since I knew her husband must have been quite old. Suddenly a very smart woman, about my age, appeared, was corralled by a bellboy and brought over to me. At first she had no notion who I was but when I mentioned Dr. Bayon's name she said, "Oh, you are the Proust lady." She asked me to come up at once, said she was having people in but could spend half an hour. So up we went and the first thing she said was, "We must have a drink." So from the little bar where I have now discovered there is always a bottle of iced pink champagne, she poured me a glass. I never had seen any before and it is utterly delectable. She says it has no alcohol. It has just the right amount to enable me to drink it quite steadily without becoming woozy. Which is lucky since I shall apparently be drinking a great deal of it in the next few weeks.

She said at once that Maurois had borrowed all of Proust's letters to Mme. Straus but that she would get them back for me. I told her that I was quite as interested in anything she could tell me about her aunt. She knew her for only a short time when she was very old, rarely saw her. But she remembered her welcoming remark. "Now we have a really charming piece of Copenhagen in the family." (It seems that Mme. Straus had a collection of hideous dark-brown or gloomy grey Copenhagen figurines of animals which she disliked but felt obliged to display because they were the gifts of the Baronne de Rothschild, a frequent caller.)

Mme. Sibilat was so excited by my knowledge about Bizet and being interested in everything that she opened a secretary and started tossing at me (it was like Alice in Wonderland flinging the pack of cards), so that they rained down on the sofa where I sat, all these magnificently bound volumes of letters and manuscripts. She said that I was the first person she had ever met who was interested or knew about them. She said she wanted to sell them, that she had given four Bizet operas in manuscript to the Nationale, that they hadn't thanked her so she would never again give them anything. She has given the score of *Carmen* to be sold for the blind and she is going to leave all her money to the American Hospital because they saved her life there.

She is Danish by birth, but is the most uninhibited type I ever met. She's awfully good and kind and appealing, quite intelligent though almost wholly uneducated and mad in an agreeable way. She at once told me all about the horrors of her husband's having been taken by the French Gestapo (the Germans left him alone and even paid the royalties on *Carmen* throughout the occupation). He was ill for twenty months after suffering a stroke during his twenty-four hours in prison and then died at the age of eighty-three. She had a complete nervous collapse — wouldn't wash, wouldn't dress, wouldn't get out of bed or eat. But after nine months in the American Hospital she is reasonably recovered and I really think that having me come along to interest her and take her mind off herself is a godsend.

About half an hour after I arrived she decided I looked just like her dear old friend Maxine Elliott who had *"le troisième oeil"* and she could tell that I have. Why not? Maybe I do. She then asked if I had a dinner engagement, and if not would I stay? I didn't have, but even if I had it would have gone by the board. At this point characters started straying into the apartment which has five or six rooms — waiters passing the champagne, the *maître d'hôtel,* a Dominican father with pink champagne in hand, the president of the Jockey Club, a Count or Duke de Cambacérès and two colossal, aged but beautiful Norwegian generals.

The dinner consisted of pearl-grey caviar, a rack of baby lamb with fresh peas, asparagus with mousseline sauce, wonderful cheese and chocolate cream-puffs. The wines were Bollinger 1929, Richebourg 1921 and Musigny 1921. The cigars were Romeo and Juliet which I haven't seen since father died. I was almost tempted to smoke one . . . But you can't imagine what it was like to have this elegant, civilized meal after the exhausting eight-course dinners served by the *bourgeoisie* where the champagne only arrives with the *glace* and I never get enough.

Now I must tell you what it was like the next morning when I went to fetch the dozen or so volumes that Mme. Sibilat let me bring here while she is in London for a week. When I think that this is a small part of what I shall see when she returns I feel considerably bewildered. In any case, I took a big suitcase filled with tissue paper and arrived at the Athénée at about eleven in the morning. Mme. S. received me in her bedroom where she was being massaged under a very large Boucher, one of the finest "Miss O'Murphys" I've ever seen. She greeted me with, "You can know people for twenty-four years and they're never your friends and you can know someone twenty-four hours and feel as though you had known them all your life. Your coming into my life is the first good thing that has happened since the war."

I had suggested the night before when she told me that she was flying to New York this week for twenty-four hours to sign a paper and coming back to London (she has never been in a plane) that it might be wiser to have someone bring the paper to London and see her there. Why no one else had this bright idea I don't know but I suppose the doctors handle her by giving her plenty of rope. The doctor who came in to vaccinate her while I was there (a nice young man from Indiana, Bayon's assistant, who has just been taking care of Carson McCullers — a gone goose, I gather) was greatly relieved at her having decided to follow my advice. She and the doctor and I, wrapped up in numerous woolen scarves which she supplied, drank pink champagne. (The heat is turned off April first in all buildings in Paris.)

I then started to leave, but she insisted I sit with her while she took her bath which I did while she talked to me about Scandinavia and invited me to spend Christmas at the lodge in Norway belonging to one of the lovely Vikings who had been at dinner the night before.

Because I can't see Mme. Straus' letters until Mme. Maurois brings them back when Mme. S. returns from London, I have been making a rough listing of a dozen or more morocco-bound albums of letters and manuscripts that belonged to Mme. Straus. There are all of Bizet's letters to his parents from Rome — a few dozen have been published but there are hundreds; his letters to his mother-in-law, many of them written during the Commune and the Siege of Paris and all of them magnificent. There is a whole volume of Gounod's letters to Bizet; letters from Berlioz, Rossini, all the musicians of the period either to Bizet or to Fromental Halévy; dozens of letters from Maupassant to Geneviève before she married Straus, letters from Renan, Zola — practically everybody important throughout the century. For my own personal delectation there are letters from Bizet to Geneviève beginning *Plus chère baby* and the letters from him to her mother, some of them quite startling.

You will now see why I am staying the extra fortnight, I shall devote all of it to going over and listing her stuff with her. Then I will get M. Halévy to go over the whole thing and explain the references. He alone can do it. After that I shall talk to the people at Harvard or Yale about buying the whole collection.

My immediate determination to offer Harvard the first chance to buy these extraordinary letters, rather than acquiring them myself, perhaps needs some explanation. My compulsion to read other people's letters, satisfied now in my old age by the continual surprise inherent in re-reading my own, was early on a counter-part to my passion for libraries. It is a subject on which I am tempted to digress at length — the rewarding torture of working in the British Museum and the Bibliothèque Nationale; the luxurious privacy of the Boston Athenaeum; the exhaustive riches of the Library of Congress; and above all the varied splendor of the collections in the New York Public Library, the unequaled prompt courtesy which enables one to hold unique treasures in one's hand merely for the asking. Libraries are indeed the only public buildings where I feel at home, where I go first when visiting a strange city. For me libraries combine unpredictable adventure with an almost womblike sense of security.

The Widener Library at Harvard initiated me into the magic world of catalogues and stacks full of treasure hidden from the underprivileged or incurious. While a graduate student at Rad-cliffe, rejoicing in the liberty of roaming the stacks, I discovered some uncatalogued, unpublished notes of Henry Adams. Not the most important scholarly discovery in the world, it served nevertheless as a subject for my first published article in *The Atlantic Monthly* and my master's thesis at Columbia. Hence my loyalty to Harvard when I realized that Mme. Sibilat's para-noiac resentment against the Bibliothèque Nationale seemed to preclude anything more of hers going to the library that should obviously be the first choice. Unfortunately, the hoped-for ar-rangements with Harvard did not work out.

2

Magda Sibilat announced her return from London in a char-acteristic way. Some ten days after I had last seen her the con-cierge called me at about nine o'clock in the morning to announce a chasseur from the Plaza-Athénée. Could he send him up? So, ushered in by the chambermaid there appeared a small boy, done up in a be-buttoned uniform and pill-box cap with Plaza-Athénée initials. He carried a miniature hatbox proportionate to his size which he asked me to open at once so that he could take it back to refill and bring again tomorrow morning.

Inside the box, cuddled in wax-paper, were three croissants, crisp, brown, aromatic, still slightly warm from the oven. The chambermaid and I were equally astonished. Sweet butter, essential to croissants, was unobtainable in Paris except, of course, at some fantastic price on the black market. At the Ritz we had yesterday's bread toasted for breakfast, and delicious it was, even with only the few curls of butter the hotel could afford to supply. *"Je n'aime pas les croissants,"* I told the chambermaid. But I ate one and gave her two, one for her husband, the valet.

When I telephoned Mme. Sibilat to thank her she said that Mme. Maurois was bringing back the Proust-Straus letters that afternoon and would I please be there when she came. So I went, and an eye-opening encounter it was. Simone Maurois, a handsome woman whom I saw on another occasion quite spectacularly dressed in purple, dress, hat, gloves and all, was clad that rainy day in a severe, dark blue rain hat and coat which Magda did not ask her to remove. She sat, hands folded, her drab costume suggesting the uniform of a woman's military unit. The contrast between our hostess' cordiality to me and her rudeness to Mme. Maurois shocked me into silence. I just sat by while Mme. Maurois tried to persuade Magda to sell her not only the letters but all the volumes of Proust's novel as well as his earlier works, each one inscribed to Mme. Straus. Magda cut her short by saying that she had no intention of selling anything, that she was sending everything to a friend in Stockholm that very night. Disconcerted by the ease with which she lied, I could see that all my tact and energy would be required to hold her to her promise to show me all the documents and books. I therefore lunched or dined or took tea with her every day for the next three weeks.

On Sunday I even skipped my dinner with Céleste in order to accompany Magda to the races at Longchamp. She and her husband had owned a racing stable and I soon discovered that her prime interest in life was horse racing.

With an unconscious innocence she confided to me her personal history. However, now that I want to tell it I find that there are great gaps. In spite of my somewhat obsessive preoccupation with viewing her collection I realized gradually that her volatile nature bordered on the paranoiac. So I never asked her questions which would seem now to be basic.

About her family or her childhood in Denmark she never said anything. At seventeen she had married a boy the same age. They were both virgins. The unconsummated marriage was soon annulled. Six years later she married René Sibilat, who was in his early fifties. How she came to meet him, whether in Paris or in Copenhagen, I have no idea. But apparently that marriage was never consummated either. Sibilat's attachment to his mother had been such that he sat on her lap until she died shortly before his marriage. He called Magda *"mon fils"* and held her on his lap. She adored him and didn't seem to think there was anything odd about their relationship. The delicate situation of dealing tactfully with a widow only recently recovered from a breakdown caused by her husband's arrest and death was a problem I had faced. Now I needed an additional understanding of the psychology of this fifty-year-old, unconsciously sex-starved widowed virgin who had developed a kind of schoolgirl crush on me. Charming and warmhearted though she was, she was incapable of facing any reality other than the pleasures of luxurious living. I even came to wonder whether this blinding limitation might have been the indirect cause of her husband's arrest. It had to do with butter.

When I thanked her for the croissants I said I had no idea it was possible to buy sweet butter in Paris. Oh, she said, she had it all during the occupation. Because of her eighty-year-old husband's ill health she was determined he should have fresh eggs, fresh cream, and butter. So to buy it she drove twice a week to a farm outside Paris. But didn't the German sentries at the gates stop her? No, they were very nice, she said. As she spoke German and was able to tip them generously, they always permitted her to pass.

Who, in the fever of anticollaborationism following the occupation, reported her husband to the French Secret Police she apparently never found out. But obviously since she was a French citizen only by marriage it was logical that her husband would be held responsible for her behavior. On the other hand, the paying throughout the occupation of Sibilat's share of the royalties from *Carmen* — a complex inheritance from Bizet's widow, Geneviève, to her second husband, Emile Straus, to his nephew and heir, René Sibilat, to his relict, Magda — may have been attributed to collaboration. I don't know. In any case he was arrested at three o'clock one morning and brought back at midnight the following night having suffered a massive stroke. For the many months he lived he could speak only one word, "*jamais.*" As far as I could tell she felt no guilt on any level, but developed an intense hatred of the French. Her rudeness to Mme. Maurois was no doubt an expression of her deep resentment against the whole French establishment.

Each day at Magda's I worked on collating the manuscript of Proust's letters to Mme. Straus with the published version. Actually it was a far less important job than I had anticipated. I was able to correct several misreadings of Proust's handwriting wrongly transcribed in the published text, but the changes were only of academic interest. More illuminating were the identities of various X's, Y's, and Z's. But a number of those I couldn't reveal because M. Halévy asked me not to. He thought that the feelings of their living heirs might be injured by Proust's mocking comments on their relatives.

3

My time, however, was not squandered. Indeed Magda's interruptions of my work led in their indirect, wandering way to the discovery of further treasure, actually via the croissants. In an attempt to stall the matutinal offering, I asked whether this gift wasn't an inconvenience. Not at all, she said. The cook who was also caretaker of her apartment in the avenue d'Iéna baked them and brought them to her every morning. She had not disposed of the apartment because she didn't know what to do about the library, which contained all of Mme. Straus' books as well as her father's and Bizet's. Unaware of the interest and significance of the printed books as opposed to the manuscripts, she prized the library simply as part of her inheritance. She had never looked at the books. Even before seeing them I was afraid that they would be scattered far and wide. Ignorant of the financial value of a complete set of inscribed Gide first editions, she had the day before, with typical spontaneous generosity, presented four of the volumes as a gift to the president of a Scandinavian steamship company, owner of a racing stable. The letters she had brought to the hotel were in a different category. They had a personal emotional significance because of their association value. Her husband had himself inserted all of them into their splendidly bound albums, ignoring any chronology but making use of tabs that precluded any injury to the letters.

Magda's procrastination in telling me about the existence of the books sprang not solely from ignorance of their scope and value. She knew well enough that I would want to see them. But the very thought of again setting foot in that unheated apartment where her husband had died was more than she could bear. She was greatly relieved, therefore, when I said I had no objection to going alone. So ten days before I had to leave Paris I saw for the first time the library of thousands of books, documents, journals, and magazines where I would eventually spend several freezing weeks.

The door to the apartment in the pretentiously elegant belle époque building was opened for me by Marie, a tiny, wizened old woman, the creator of the croissants. She tried to make polite conversation, but I was not responsive. For the instant I entered the foyer which she had lighted for me, my eye fell on the framed manuscript of Bizet's "*Habanera.*" There it was — just an ordinary piece of paper on which were written the words of that perfect song known throughout the world.

> *L'amour est enfant de Bohême . . .*
> *Il ne connût jamais de loi* [sic]
> *Si tu ne m'aimes pas je t'aime! . . .*
> *Si tu m'aimes . . . tant pis pour toi! . . .* [sic]

Writing from hindsight, as I do today, I would like to believe that the words Bizet wrote vertically along the margin — *"Prière de ne rien changer de tout cela"* — were the first hint I had of the tragedy they foretold. But that would be quite untrue. I only glanced at the manuscript that day. I do remember, though, a sense of sadness at seeing so personal and unique a creation neglected in the crowded luxury of the empty apartment.

Marie led me through the vast salon, furnished in what may well have been original examples of the Louis XV replicas in my rooms at the Ritz. Adjoining the salon was the library, equally vast, lined floor-to-ceiling with bookshelves. I can't now remember the sequence of my reactions on first seeing those books. Surprise, of course, for I had no idea that there were thousands. Nor at that time did the name of Mme. Straus' father, Fromental Halévy, mean anything to me other than his identity as composer of *La Juive.* That he had been director of the Opéra, professor at the Conservatoire, and Permanent Secretary of the Académie des Beaux Arts, I learned only later. These positions brought him into active touch with the most distinguished painters, composers, and writers in France. At random as I wandered past the shelves I picked up a first edition of Renan's *La Vie de Jésus* with six important letters to his colleagues at the Collège de France inserted; a charmingly bound copy of Alphonse Daudet's *L'Arlésienne* with an inscription praising Bizet's music for the play; bound manuscripts of novels by Bourget inscribed to Mme. Straus; albums of original drawings by Forain. I soon realized that here in this room I was standing in the midst of documentation that revealed a whole cross section of the artistic and social worlds of nineteenth-century France. To scatter this treasure would be a sin against scholarship. Then and there I made up my mind to prevent such a disaster.

How to proceed stymied me at first. I didn't know how to impress Magda with the scholarly significance of her possessions during the few days I had left in Paris. But the chameleonlike side of my nature fortunately took over. I ceased being a *femme de lettres,* a potential biographer, and reverted to the practical status of merchant's daughter. The library people at Harvard had made an offer which Magda thought was too low for some of the Proust material. Now the unexpected discovery of this additional treasure changed the nature of any financial arrangement. No list or catalogue of the library existed, or if it did Magda didn't know its whereabouts. I therefore offered to come back and list everything for her after my book was published at the end of the year. But I made a condition. She must promise not to give away or sell anything in my absence, to give me a lien on the whole collection. My relief was great when she not only agreed to have this arrangement recorded in a letter, but even accepted as deputy in my absence the attractive and understanding American lawyer whom I brought in to draw up the rather questionably legal agreement.

The thought of her loneliness after I left worried me. For I was really fond of her and feared that the depressive cycle of her illness might recur if she were alone too much. She seemed to have no close friends in Paris so I suggested introducing her to friends of mine. My women friends, all French, were no use because of her paranoia about French people. And obviously the men would have to be carefully selected. So I mentioned Russell Page, now an internationally known landscape gardener, then the head of the landscaping division of the famous nursery and seed firm, Vilmorin — a gentle, handsome, intelligent charmer whom I first met during the war when we were both attached to the Office of War Information. He was what we called a "British spy" and I a scriptwriter for a BBC program, "Answering You." At first Russell had seemed to me like a character in one of Maurice Baring's low-key but romantic novels, but he turned out to be far more interesting. And I knew he would be kind to Magda and patient with her.

"How old is he?" she wanted to know. About forty, I thought. No, that was too young. She only liked older men. Then I suggested Sherry Mangan, also kind, but eccentric enough himself to be amused by a certain degree of madness in others. He was handsome, blond, blue-eyed, lace-curtain Irish, Harvard, a Luce journalist, a poet in the classic vein, and an active Trotsky-ite. Needless to say I disclosed to Magda only his more conventional attributes. But when I had to admit that he was no older than we were, she rejected him, too. As a last resort I mentioned Antoine.

Although I had little faith in his capacity to help me keep track of her condition while I was away, he was, after all, the right age. Besides he was endlessly curious about her, always urging me to introduce him. So I told her I had a seventy-year-old friend whom she might like, Prince Antoine Bibesco. "A Rumanian!" she practically spat out, and then in a funny sing-song voice recited a stanza which I believe is well known but which I had never heard.

Les hommes sans honneur
Les femmes sans pudeur
Les fruits sans saveur
Les fleurs sans odeur
C'est la Roumanie!

I did not report to Antoine her reaction to his name and had to leave Paris knowing that there was no way of keeping track of Magda while I was in Ashfield devoting my time to the formidable task of preparing for the press the final version of *Letters of Marcel Proust*. But I had the satisfaction of a valid reason for returning to Paris before the year was over.

Chapter 12

THE CRISIS, short-lived but acute, that initiated my return
to France in December 1948 on the S.S. *America* now appears symbolic of the discomfiture and discomfort that were to
serve as background to my labors.

The episode of the lost briefcase happened because my car had
traveled with me on the ship. Just before landing, the baggage
master assured me that he himself would pack all my luggage
into the car on shipboard, thereby making it possible for the
customs to pass everything through at once. This he appeared
to have done. But when I counted the pieces after landing, one
was missing.

"For the first time in my life," I wrote my mother from Paris,
"I let my despatch case with all my Proust research out of my
hands. I was convinced it was on the ship but they couldn't find
it. So for two days I thought my life's work was lost. Then the
case was found and deposited at Southampton. But by that time
I had so impressed upon the authorities the rarity and uniqueness
of the contents that the British customs authorities refused to let
it be flown here from Southampton until it had been examined
by the Ministry of Fine Arts. So now it is being held at the

Customs in Southampton, where it is safe, until the next American ship comes in when it will be sent here to the Ritz from Le Havre by personal courier. I must say that both the baggage master on the ship and the one here (who received a bottle of whiskey for his efforts) were unbelievably imaginative and efficient. They were both German, as were most of the crew, and whatever one may say against the Germans, they do have feelings about scholarship and they are efficient."

Any anxiety about my wandering papers was overshadowed by the shock of my first encounter with Magda. She had not written during my six months' absence. But in July I had news of her in a letter from Francis Steegmuller. He was writing a life of Maupassant and wanted to see his letters to Mme. Straus in Magda's possession. I gave him a letter of introduction to her.

"Her messages to you," he wrote, "are that she will write as soon as she is settled in Aix and that I should send you her love — a difficult thing for me to do in a letter since there seems to me to be so very much of it. She is your adorer, as you doubtless know. She gave me champagne and let me take the Maupassant letters home to copy. I returned them today and found her suffering from hay fever, but nevertheless still vivacious. She wept a bit when speaking of her husband, but seemed otherwise not 'out of the ordinary' except in the best possible ways. Among the milder of her expressed opinions about you was that you would make a good President of the United States — 'Then we'd all have fun.'"

But there was no fun that bleak day in December when I walked into Magda's room at the Plaza-Athénée. Instead of the chic, gay, fastidious woman I had known there lay in her bed a shrunken little figure in a soiled nightgown, face drawn and smudged, hair in a tangle. The bare, scarred wall beside her bed from which Boucher's bouncy "Miss O'Murphy" had dominated the room now served as fitting background for the distraught figure lying there like a suitable subject for Fuseli. She greeted me in tears, said I was the first person she had seen in three months except for doctors, nurses, and her masseuse. The poor woman suffered a total nervous breakdown in August and had left the American Hospital only three days earlier. Terror, because her income had shrunk to such an extent that she couldn't envisage any future, had reduced her to this pitiful state. She couldn't sleep, she said, or eat, or get out of bed to bathe except on the days the masseuse came. She left the hospital only because Dr. Bayon had gone back to the States. Whether her financial situation was really as desperate as she thought I have never known. But a look around the apartment showed that the Boucher was not the only sacrifice to ready money. A blank hole in the ceiling replaced the delicate ormolu chandelier studded with little Dresden china flowers I had found so charming. Gone was a rare and beautiful Prud'hon drawing. The pretty eighteenth-century cabinet was bereft of its choice bibelots. Pushed in a corner, as though for punishment, stood the little bar on wheels — no ice, no pink champagne.

Magda was too excited at seeing me to talk coherently. And her joy at my return, her affection for me were really touching. However, I was frightened by her conviction that by converting her library into American dollars I alone could save her life. Not that I ever doubted the salability of the manuscripts. I had looked forward to spreading the task of listing the contents of the library over a long enough time to enjoy examining them. But after spending several hours with her during the next few days it became clear that from her point of view the actual physical possession of dollars that she could hold in her hand was the only possible cure for her illness. I tried to persuade her to sell the ten-room avenue d'Iéna apartment, but her insistence that the furniture must be included in the sale, her refusal to reduce the fantastically high price she was asking made this arrangement impossible.

On my second or third visit I asked her to see a psychiatrist, but in her mind they were all witch doctors. The only cure, she kept saying, was dollars. So because the Proust letters had all been published I overcame my dislike of separating them from the rest of the collection. I sold them to an American living in Paris, a person who would be generous about showing them to scholars. The actual physical impact of the dollar bills, an amount which in the past she would have regarded as negligible, was indeed therapeutic. She started eating a little, washing occasionally and expressing her gratitude to me in a way that was irresistible. Obviously, all I could do was postpone my research for the Proust biography, which I still intended writing, to devote my time to making at least a sketchy catalogue of the books in the library at once. During the summer I had told the people at Yale about the collection, and they were optimistic about finding a donor to buy it for them. But I had not foreseen the complications that would inevitably ensue, the length of time such negotiations normally require.

There was no delay, however, in my own efforts to get the work underway. Less than a week after I landed, Liliane Yacoël and I started our labors in the avenue d'Iéna apartment to which Magda had given me a key. There was no Marie to let us in — no heat, almost no light, no dust covers on the brocaded fauteuils, dust lying thick on all the tables, and worst of all on the books. But the very discomfort was a stimulus. The sooner we adjusted ourselves to it, the quicker the job would be done. So we agreed on a method. Liliane sat at a desk and wrote down the necessary details about the books as I took them, one by one, off the shelves and replaced them in spite of the dust, which was a double problem. Not only did it make me sneeze a great deal but I couldn't bear the inefficiency of not cleaning the shelves and books. The water in the apartment was turned off so I couln't even wash my hands. The white cotton gloves acquired after the first day solved that problem.

But the main obstacle was the few hours a day we could tolerate the cold and the meager lighting. I wouldn't have had the physical stamina to steal time to examine the treasures at all carefully even if I had not been driven by such a sense of urgency. This was enhanced by my daily visits to Magda to report progress. She had no understanding or interest in the procedure, and her depression continued. She still claimed that she neither slept nor ate except for the tidbits I brought to tempt her. "Her melancholia is beginning to get me down," I wrote home at the end of the month, "and I know there will be no turning point until she is convinced that money is coming in."

2

Were I to depend solely on my memory for this period I would give the false impression that discomfort, anxiety, and tension existed only in the microcosm of the Plaza-Athénée and the avenue d'Iéna. But as I now re-read the letters I wrote that winter I see that my situation was only a reflection of the climate of Paris, economically, socially, and meteorologically. Two days before Christmas I wrote to my mother:

> No one in America can picture the cold in the houses here and what it does to you. What I would do without these lovely rooms with really warm radiators and wood fires I don't know. I hope you realize how grateful I am to you for making it possible for me to come back to the Ritz.
>
> The thermometer doesn't go much below 32° Fahrenheit, but the dampness is like an evil, malignant force that you can't escape and the effect of which you don't realize until you start sneezing like mad and choking up. The museums and theatres are draughty and I haven't

even been tempted to walk in the streets and look in the windows . . .

The rare days it is light outdoors the sun doesn't shine until noon and only stays out until four. But most days we are shrouded in fog and it is barely possible to see even with street lamps that are about as adequate as the lights in the N.Y. subway . . . Two days a week the electricity is off from nine to five. This arrangement holds for every *arrondissement* so that all the workshops are shut those two days. You can imagine what that does to the morale of the people. There is no coal to be bought (one of the first things the concierge asked me was whether I had brought any briquettes this time). The gas and electric restrictions are so severe that nobody, not even rich people, can afford to keep more than one room in a house heated. The damp cold in the old houses penetrates even into the heated rooms. I manage to stay well as long as I don't get chilled, but you never know you're chilled until you start sneezing. Then you rush home to bed, hot-water bottle and brandy to avoid succumbing to the prevalent flu epidemic.

In spite of the negative conditions the list was typed and sent off to Yale just a month after Liliane and I started our daily sessions at the avenue d'Iéna. But the release from this labor did not leave me free to continue my research on Proust as I had hoped. For a chapter on his relation to his mother and his illness, I wanted to read the works on asthma, on neuroses and neurology that he himself read. Also I wanted to find the articles by Marcel's father based originally on his journey to Persia to investigate a cholera epidemic and on the establishing of the cordon sanitaire. Most of them were in official reports but two appeared in *La Revue des Deux Mondes* in the early nineties at the time Marcel was contributing to the little magazine, *Le*

Banquet, the tales later to appear in *Les Plaisirs et les jours.* I
had a feeling that Dr. Proust might well have asked his writer-son
to collaborate with him or perhaps even revise. Later on under
more felicitous conditions I was able to confirm my suspicion.
There are certainly echoes of Marcel in the following example.
A passage in *Les Plaisirs et les jours* opens with the sentences
"Today's paradoxes are tomorrow's prejudices. The dullest and
most unpleasant of today's prejudices achieve a momentary novelty when fashion lends them its fragile favour." In an article
entitled "Etudes de Hygiène" by Dr. Adrien Proust in *La Revue
des Deux Mondes,* December 1893, the following sentence appears: "The time has perhaps come to discuss many opinions
that fluctuate between young paradoxes and old prejudices."

But at that time when I most wanted to read the medical material, red tape, the weather, the heating, and lighting restrictions
interfered. The books were all available in the library of the
Faculté de Médicine. But that is a formidable fortress. Even
with the aid of Liliane's father, a distinguished heart specialist
and a member of the faculty, days passed before an alien lay
person could receive permission to work in the library, which was
open only from one to seven without light or heat. And while
I was deciding whether to risk my own health in an effort to
study the intricacies of Proust's, a new frustration occurred.

The donor for whom Yale had hoped did not materialize,
largely because he felt that the contents of the library were too
special, of interest only in France. Of the details following this
disappointment I have very little recollection and too few *aides-
mémoires.* Suffice it to say that Magda gave to the Bibliothèque
Nationale, in memory of her husband, the library of printed
books she had inherited as well as a number of holograph letters
to Mme. Straus from various writers, academicians, persons
prominent in their own day but of interest only to specialists.
For the immensely valuable Bizet-Halévy part of the collection
I paid an option of several thousand dollars. The full amount

was paid after an appraisal made on my return to New York. I borrowed the money from my mother to do this, partly so that Magda could have the reassurance of cash in hand. Also it was somewhat belatedly revealed to me by Robert, the concierge at the Ritz, who knew about the treasure, that I was mistaken in thinking that the documents Magda insisted on my keeping with me were safely stored in a locked closet in my apartment. The key, it seemed, opened all similar closets on that floor. So in order to insure the collection (she carried no insurance) it was necessary for me to have a legal claim to it.

Apart from the shock of my tardy discovery about the universal key, I have only a single concrete memory of this nerve-racking period. That is the day, just two months after my arrival, when the blue-smocked employees of the Bibliothèque arrived with a truck to pack carefully the masses of books, cartons of letters, magazines, and files in the library of the avenue d'Iéna apartment. The day after I superintended this procedure the influenza against which I had fought so hard conquered.

The attack differed in only one way from previous or subsequent attacks largely forgotten. But it was memorable. In addition to all the typical symptoms, a very high fever apparently activated a turbulence in my head. There, four *Heinzelmännchen* straight out of *Grimm's Fairy Tales* my childhood *Fräulein* used to read to me beat on my brain with tiny metal dentists' hammers. I could visualize them clearly. I don't suppose this phenomenon lasted very long, but in an earlier century I am sure it would have been diagnosed as brain fever. It was very depleting. The doctor insisted that I go south to recuperate in the sun.

The day before I departed, Magda, who had not left her room in months, dressed, did her hair, put on make-up, and came down to lunch in the Plaza-Athénée dining room. It was a gallant effort to assure me that she was on the way to recovery.

I never saw her again. She disappeared out of my life as un-

predictably as she entered it. Perhaps there is some sort of per-
verse logic in the fact that almost as much energy went into my
unsuccessful efforts to trace her whereabouts as I had expended
in the original successful search. Soon after she received the
additional payment on the collection she moved out of the Plaza-
Athénée, taking all her belongings and leaving no forwarding
address. By the time I returned to France after a year and a
half away there were no longer any clues. Her death, two or
three years later, was announced to me in a letter from a Lady
Somebody (I have forgotten her name) in London, a sister
whom Magda had never mentioned. She died in the south of
France, where she had been living in a small villa with a nurse-
companion. Poor Magda, I thought, the most urban of people,
should not have died in an ambience so remote from what she
would have chosen when I first knew her.

In my wide experience with relatives, friends, and retainers,
subject from time to time to a variety of nervous disorders,
Magda Sibilat remains the only one who, however ill and unhappy she might be, never showed a trace of meanness or aggres-
sion, unkindness or lack of generosity. I like to remember her
by a remark she once made. She was urging me to move from
the Ritz to the Plaza-Athénée. I refused, explaining that a view
of the Place Vendôme played a very important role in my life,
especially late at night and early in the morning when it was all
silent space. "Everyone should have a Place Vendôme in their
hearts," Magda said. I am afraid that she never found one.

That this frivolous, half-mad woman should have turned out
to be the catalyst for an enduring change in the pattern of my
life was an unpredictable phenomenon. Led to her by my search
for Proust letters I came away the owner of a quite different correspondence which seduced me as other people's letters so often
have. While convalescent in the south I spent most of my time
transcribing Bizet's and his wife's diaries and letters. Gradually,
the spell of reading these unpublished documents, replete, as I

soon realized, with suppressed clues to an understanding of their writers' relationships, drew me irretrievably into an exploration of their lives. Thus after spending the better part of the next decade writing *Bizet and His World,* I found that my childhood trauma had willy-nilly led me to change my profession from teacher to biographer.

Chapter 13

THREE DAYS before New Year's, 1949, twenty-four pre-publication copies of *Letters of Marcel Proust* arrived in Paris from Random House. To perceive and hold in one's hand for the first time the finished product of so many years of work would seem to readers a sufficiently exciting event to counteract the past troubles and frustrations inherent in the composition of any serious work. But writers know this is not true. "For a moment I was really thrilled," I wrote to my mother. "It really is a very handsome book. But then, after admiring the illustrations — very well reproduced — I started looking at the text. With my fatal eye, I found half a dozen mistakes which I daresay no one else will notice but which shifted my interest on to the next book in which I trust there will be none." But mistakes and all, I did find considerable satisfaction in being able to send as New Year's gifts twenty inscribed copies to the letter-writers themselves and to the other people who were so helpful to me.

To say that the impact of the book itself on the recipients was impressive is not vainglorious. Compared even to the French edition of Proust's correspondence, paperbound, printed on poor paper, the purely physical aspect of this translation was indeed splendid. I still treasure the thank you letters from Proust's friends, especially those from the Comte Robert de Billy and the Duchesse de Clermont-Tonnerre, written in English. Indeed it is to the Duchesse that I owe by far the most essentially Proustian of all my encounters — Proustian in the sense that he could somehow have fitted it into *Le Temps retrouvé*.

When I returned to Paris after two months in the south, Jenny Bradley told me that Mme. de Clermont-Tonnerre had asked her to arrange an appointment with the Comtesse Greffulhe, who would like to discuss with me a possible biography of her cousin, Robert de Montesquiou. To my knowledge no letters from Proust to the Comtesse have ever been published. Indeed I doubt whether she even saved them. For this reason I had no occasion to include her in my researches. I knew of Proust's lifelong admiration of her beauty, even after he no longer saw her, and of his incorporation of one or two details of her coiffure and toilette into his descriptions of the Guermantes ladies. That she had actually survived him surprised me only less than her interest at the age of ninety in choosing an unknown American as possible biographer of her notorious cousin, whose devotion to her had been such that she was the only person with whom he never quarreled.

The details leading to my interview with the Comtesse Greffulhe I have never known. Probably the Duchesse, who was her close friend as well as relative (the Comtesse' daughter was married to Mme. de Clermont-Tonnerre's brother, the Duc de Gramont), had liked the brief essay on Montesquiou in my book and had shown it or read it to Mme. Greffulhe. In any case the invitation was hardly one I would want to refuse in spite of the trepidation it aroused in me. Under no circumstances would I consider writing a life of Montesquiou, that loathsome character, arrogant nobleman, notorious in his lifetime as a pretentious poet and aesthete, become posthumously immortal as the Baron de Charlus. Translating Proust's egregiously flattering letters to him was one of the few distasteful elements of my work. Knowing as little as I did about the beautiful cousin who in her old age wished to revive his memory, I felt ill prepared to deny her request graciously. Needing some sort of guide, I turned back to Mme. de Clermont-Tonnerre's memoirs, which I had read only cursorily several years earlier. Here is her description, written in the 1920s, of the great lady on whose doorstep I was soon to stand, eager but timorous.

The Comtesse Greffulhe is always beautiful and always everywhere. But it would be a mistake to think that her life was merely the pursuit of pleasure. One can't just enjoy one's self and be the most beautiful lady of France — not only is she beautiful, but she is a lady . . .

Preferring the privacy of her own house in the rue d'Astorg and at Bois-Boudran in the country, the Comtesse Greffulhe never dined out except at the British Embassy. When Edward VII came to Paris he dined informally at her house. After a restricted youth — she was forced to spend many evenings playing piquet with her highly conventional parents-in-law — she longed for the pleasure of more intellectual society. So she set herself to attracting musicians, scholars, physicists, chemists, doctors.

Then something remarkable happened. These scientists, invited at the most improbable hours — half past eight or nine in the evening — came, and in the company of the Comtesse Greffulhe talked about things she couldn't possibly understand. They knew it, and so did she. But both talkers and listener were enchanted with each other by a more subtle phenomenon than outright understanding. Between the scholar and the beautiful lady there existed a felicitous exchange, almost mystical.

She perceived the scale and power of the scientific experiments that were discussed in her presence, and the scientists were imbued in the radiance of her dark eyes and her smile . . .

The magic of her eyes also moved Marcel Proust, who when he was only twenty-two described his first, long-desired glimpse of her in a letter to Montesquiou: ". . . All the mystery of her beauty is in the brilliance, the enigma of her eyes. I have never seen such a beautiful woman. But I did not ask for an introduction . . . I think talking to her might disturb and embarrass me." Like Proust I half dreaded our conversation; like him, like her intellectual admirers, I too found her eyes uniquely magnetic. Remembering them has led me chronologically awry.

2

One April afternoon Liliane and I stood on the doorstep of number 10 rue d'Astorg, one of the great Greffulhe family mansions clustered in parklike grounds. (They were all destroyed in 1975 to make way for an insurance company, Caisses Centrales de la Mutualité Agricole.) The door was opened by a plump, balding, youngish man who introduced himself as the Comtesse' secretary. Something eunuchlike in his gracious manner belied his status, for his name, which I can't remember exactly — Fenélon? d'Alembert? — identified him as a member of one of the great ancient families of France.

When I try to recall my impressions as he led us through one huge salon after another there pops into my mind a line from *The Bohemian Girl,* an opera which fascinated me in my childhood and which I can't have thought of in seventy years: "I dreamt I dwelt in marble halls." But our progress through those pillared halls gradually took on the quality, not of a dream but a vacuous night-mare. They were totally bare. Not a single piece of furniture re-lieved the stark pallor of the marble. Nothing of the past décor remained except the painted ceilings — sky blue, mottled with white clouds, like the ceilings of the Ritz dining rooms in Paris and London. Our passage through three or four of these ghostly salons led to a smaller room — octagonal or circular, as I remem-ber it — sparsely furnished with a very large round table, a few chairs, and, on an easel, a three-quarter-length portrait of the Abbé Mugnier, painted, we were informed, by the Comtesse herself. While the secretary went to inform Madame of our ar-rival, I turned back the cover of a parchment-bound quarto lying on the table and was confronted with the heroic-size handwriting of a lengthy inscription to Mme. Greffulhe signed "Gabriele d'Annunzio." The nature of the text I never discovered, for after only a few minutes the secretary returned. He led us back to the service wing into a tiny elevator. During the occupation, he explained, it had been impossible to heat the quarters the Germans had assigned to Mme. Greffulhe, so she moved up into the small maids' rooms in the attic. Here she found herself so comfortable that she chose to live there permanently. As we emerged from the confines of the creaking little elevator into a dimly lighted hall, we were greeted by Mme. Greffulhe's eighty-five-year-old unmarried sister, the Princesse de Caraman-Chimay. A formidable figure, masively tall and broad, a dark wig framing her wide face, she greeted us most graciously. A few steps be-hind her stood her maid, equally massive and dressed like her mistress in a heavy dark brown wool garment and beaming with pleasure while the Princesse explained how few visitors her sister now received and how pleased she was that we could come. Ushering us into the Comtesse' boudoir she of necessity with-drew. The size of the room would hardly have permitted the simultaneous presence of my own sizable build and her massive shape. Besides two chairs, it contained an ornate little cast-iron stove called a *salamandre* and a small table next to a chaise longue in which the Comtesse was propped up by a number of cushions. What first caught my eye, I must admit, even before she greeted us, was the exquisitely hand-quilted white satin lap robe drawn over her knees. In contrast to this glossy anachronism from pre-war days, the folds of a dull green machine-knit sweater — the kind concierges wear — and a flamboyant silk scarf enveloped her small frail body. "Henna" was the term we used to describe the color of her dyed hair in the days when the only alternative shade was "strawberry blonde." But in no way did it detract from the still-beautiful bony structure of her parchmentlike face. Her hands were covered by a pair of little white cotton gloves. These she did not remove until I was leaving. Then, there was disclosed a huge cabochon emerald ring, too heavy a burden, I thought, for the frail hand she gave me in farewell.

Wondering as I write why these external, material details form such a clear picture in my memory, it occurs to me that the surprise of finding this heroine of Proust's imagination in so unexpected an ambience inhibited my perceiving its larger significance. Now, however, I can see that the contrast of the ugly green ersatz fabric cardigan with the pristine elegance of the white satin quilt and the costly emerald ring was a palpable symbol of the paradox to which time and history had reduced her way of living.

Only after sitting down to face the Comtesse could I observe the famous eyes, which Montesquiou described as "like black fireflies" and another admirer compared to "dark mineral, like agates or topazes." Although no longer shining nor evocative of any mineral, precious or semiprecious, the color of her eyes was unique. Looking into them kindled my memory of the dark purple brown-tinged petals of a rarely seen pansy. Their very beauty, their depth, at first silenced me. But it soon became clear that her will power was stronger than her physique and that I must come to the point as soon as possible.

Soon after the *politesses* were over, I brought up the subject of Montesquiou. I was afraid, I said, that she didn't perhaps realize that although M. de Montesquiou had many years ago lectured in the United States, he was no longer known to the new generation of publishers who would be unlikely to welcome a book about him. In any case, I did not feel that I was a suitable choice as his biographer. The picture I would draw would not please the family. "Not at all," said Mme. Greffulhe in her exquisite, barely accented English. "I was fond of Robert and he was devoted to me. But that didn't blind me to his faults. The very last thing he did we none of us could understand. It shocked us very much that he chose to be buried at Versailles next to that thief Yturri instead of in the Merovingian cemetery with his own family."

Gabriel d'Yturri, Montesquiou's *soi-disant* secretary, companion, and adored and adoring slave for many years, was a South American of questionable background. Some biographers believe that they met at an exhibition of Whistler's paintings. But many of his contemporaries thought that the Comte had plucked him from behind a counter in the Louvre department store. "I didn't know he was a thief," I said. "I thought he was just a counter-bounder. That's how I've heard him described."

"I have good proof of his thievery," she went on. "You know Whistler's portrait of Robert. You must have seen it in New York [in the Frick Collection]. You know the long cape folded over his arm. Well, that was my chinchilla cape. Robert wanted something of mine to be in the portrait. So because it was light to hold I loaned it to him. About a year or so later when I was sure the portrait must be completed I asked Robert to return my cape. 'But, my dear,' he said, 'you must have forgotten. I gave it to Yturri to bring back to you six months ago.' Not that he always stole for himself. Often if Robert admired some small object in a house they visited — a piece of jade or porcelain perhaps — Yturri somehow managed to lay hands on it and present it as a gift to Robert."

At this point she closed her eyes and fell into a little catnap out of which she emerged in a few minutes, coherent and lively. "Robert didn't always approve of me. He and my mother-in-law, who used to watch from the house over there to see who my guests were, thought it was shocking of me to enjoy the company of radicals like Aristide Briand and scentists like M. Branly." (If while living one year in the Quai Branly I had not been curious about the name I would not have known that Edouard Branly, a physician, was the inventor, among other things, of the radio-conductor, an essential part of wireless telegraphy.)

"I take it that your cousin didn't bring M. Proust here in that company."

"No," she said, "as a favor to Robert I invited him a few times to soirées where he could mingle with the sort of people he wanted to meet. Robert liked him and was one of the first to believe in his talent."

"You didn't like him?" I asked.

"No," she said, "I didn't like him. His sticky flattery was not to my taste. There was something I found unattractive about him. And then there was the nonsense about my photograph, pestering Robert to get one from me. In those days, Madame, photographs were considered private and intimate. One didn't give them to outsiders. The last time I saw him was at my daughter's wedding to Guiche, who was devoted to Proust. Even there he mentioned the photograph. He was tiresome. But of course, I never saw him after he turned out to be the genius Robert predicted."

Poor Marcel! A favorite in so many salons, rejected by the one woman whose beauty he cherished all his life and whose name, when mentioned today, is usually associated with his.

While I have been writing about Mme. Greffulhe there has lain in front of me on my desk a piece of ordinary pad-paper on which are inscribed in pencil in the exaggeratedly large hand-writing of diminished vision the following words:

Panse chaque blessure
Dompte chaque tourment.
Ecrit à mon sujet par Robert de Montesquiou.
(Heal every wound
Conquer every trouble.
Written about me by Robert de Montesquiou.)

How or why I should have forgotten the existence of this illuminating scrap of paper I don't know. Nor can I even now
recall the relevant moment in our conversation when she wrote
it out for me. It was filed with a letter from her thanking me
for the copy I sent her of *Letters of Marcel Proust.* But that letter, in beautiful, compact formal handwriting, was obviously
penned by her aristocratic secretary.

Chapter 14

I F T H E R E S E A R C H for Proust's letters led to a change of direc-
tion in my life, the publication of the work initiated an unpredictable transformation in Céleste's. "This is the first time in my
life I have wished I were Céleste Albaret," Proust's niece Mme.
Mante wrote in a postscript to her thank you letter for the book.
This statement was prompted, of course, by my dedication of
the book to Céleste, which revealed to many of Proust's friends
and admirers that she was still alive and became the impetus
of her gradual rise from humble hotelkeeper to landowner and
author.

During the year and a half I was away from Paris the details
of her changing social status were reported to me in letters.
Sometimes she herself wrote. More often she dictated letters to
her daughter. That so charming and beautiful a girl might be
fated to earn her living indefinitely as a file clerk in the dreary
town hall of the sixth *arrondissement* bothered me from the
time I first met her. I therefore arranged to have her learn typing,
shorthand, and English, which by 1950 she could read well
enough to facilitate my side of the correspondence.

The first intimations of the new developments in Céleste's

social life were reported to me as early as June 1949. "Mme
Schiff's nephew, Major Behrens, came to see *Maman* again,"
Odile wrote. "He was accompanied by Prince Paul of Yugo-
slavia and his son. (Coincidence — the Prince Bibesco had been
here the same day in the morning.) I think *Maman* is going to
visit Mme Schiff the 22nd of June.

"M Maurois has sent his book on Proust to *Maman,* but I
have not yet had time to read it."

Early in January 1950, Odile wrote that "Mme Mante came
to see *Maman* the evening of last 18 November to invite her to
a mass which was celebrated the next day in memory of her
uncle at the Dominican Chapel, Faubourg St. Honoré. The
mass was read by the Rev. Father Couturier (a Dominican
Father, very worldly, very cultivated). Only Mme Mante, her
younger daughter, *Maman* and Mme Maurois were present.
After the service, Mme Mante, her daughter and *Maman* went
to the cemetery in Mme Mante's car, the latter having bought
flowers for *Maman* to put on the grave. Afterwards she came
back here and took a cup of coffee.

"Mme Mante told *Maman* she would do everything to please
her and to help me in every way possible. She approved of my
learning stenography, shorthand and English and of my going to
England. *Maman* told her about everything you have done for
me. She also said that a friendship like yours has been such a
comfort that it always seems to her that Marcel Proust had sent
you from above. For he always wanted her to be happy after he
was gone and that had not happened."

Within a week of her visit Mme. Mante sent her *homme
d'affaires* to prove her intention of easing Céleste's life by arranging for an annuity. Soon after this, Proust's niece paid
Céleste a second visit. "She came to announce to *Maman* the
marriage of her daughter Dominique (the oldest, 20) to the
Comte de Puységur. The marriage will be celebrated 9 Feb. and
she invited *Maman* and me to come to the wedding and to the

house afterwards! The dedication of your book to *Maman* has certainly had reverberations."

Céleste and Odile attended the wedding ceremony which, Odile wrote me, took place at Notre-Dame de Grâce church in Passy: "The mass was celebrated by Father Couturier. The floral decorations in the church and the bride's gown made a very cinematographic effect. The weather was horrible but there were very many, very elegant guests. Dr. Le Masle did not come. On the way out *Maman* met Maurice Rostand [son of Edmond Rostand], and both of them were really glad to see each other."

A Belgian lady, author of a book on Proust, accompanied the Albarets to the wedding. Mme. Léa François had for several months been paying Céleste visits as a result of which she and Odile were invited to go to Liège a week after the wedding for the opening of a Proust exhibition. Mme. François came to Paris to drive her guests to Liège. Odile's account of that adventure suggests that she was a reporter *manquée*:

> Our journey to Belgium was very pleasant. Mme François and her daughter were most cordial and *Maman* was *très entourée et fêtée*. The day after our arrival Mme François gave a "cocktail" in honor of *Maman* in her apartment. The important Brussels papers sent reporters and *Maman's* talk was taped for radio. The next day was the preview of the Proust exhibition at Liège. Several gentlemen spoke and some of Reynaldo Hahn's and Bizet's music was played. Then Mme François said a few words and asked *Maman* to tell some of her recollections of life at Marcel Proust's. She was very much moved and ended by saying that "for her Proust died every day because he had given her the best of herself." The whole audience shared her emotion and there was much applause.
>
> Mme Mante, her son and her younger daughter were there. Mme Mante was seated in the place of honor and

Maman was on her right!!! Before we left *Maman* was presented a silver platter in the center of which were engraved the words "To Céleste Albaret with thanks for sharing her memories at the opening of the Marcel Proust exhibition, Liège, February 20, 1950." *Maman* was very much touched by this . . .

Tributes continued: "Two weeks ago the Comtesse de Chambrun [Pierre Laval's daughter] came to tell *Maman* that Paul Morand, who had a copy of his *Le Visiteur du soir* specially printed for her, was passing through Paris and would like to see her at the Comtesse' house. *Maman* went. Docteur Le Masle was there, too. *Maman* was deeply moved by Paul Morand's gracious welcome and the way he talked to her about the past."

My interest in the past having receded from Proust to Bizet, it was inevitable that during my brief stays in Paris in the early fifties I saw Céleste only infrequently. Both of our social worlds had changed. When I wasn't working in the music division of the Bibliothèque Nationale (blessedly endowed with open stacks and a card catalogue), I was meeting musicologists, opera people, and members of Bizet's mother's family, the Delsartes. If I stopped by at Céleste's when I had time, I was likely to find her sitting for her portrait by a sculptress, being interviewed by journalists, or entertaining guests whose company I could live without. The family atmosphere which I had enjoyed, that was so helpful to me in my Proust work, had evaporated. Our correspondence dwindled accordingly. But in the early fifties I did receive rewarding if embarrassingly emotional expressions of gratitude informing me that Odile's new skills had brought her a splendid position. She was now secretary to a municipal councilor whose office was in the Hôtel de Ville. In 1955 she married her employer's son. Odile's marriage coincided, more or less, with an even more drastic change in the life of the Albaret family.

2

The always devoted Robert Le Masle arranged somehow for Céleste to sell the hotel and become caretaker of the Ravel museum in Montfort-l'Amaury, a charming village about an hour from Paris. My first visit to Céleste in her new persona as guardian of Ravel's memory in his home gave me an unforgettable moment of pure joy. To see her, her sister Marie, and Odilon transferred from their crowded, dark surroundings into this light, sunny, attractive house with a balcony giving onto a circular flower garden seemed like a fairy tale with a happy ending come true. Actually for Céleste it was only the beginning of further upward reaches which Odilon was not to share.

His terminal illness was obvious, but he was cheerful and happy. Céleste's erstwhile superior attitude toward him had changed into tenderness. There was no bickering. She even allowed him to repeat his redundant Proust anecdotes without interruption. "She tends me like one of her little chickens," he said. At lunch a gigot replaced the customary chicken and the subject of conversation took on a new tone.

Although Proust had never known Ravel personally, his music was sometimes included in the programs of the quartet that performed privately in his apartment, and indeed Ravel's *Pavane pour une Infante défunte* had been played at Proust's funeral. Céleste's interest, however, was in the living Ravel, the composer's brother who was responsible for the management of the museum. Her relationship with Maurice Ravel's heir had become quite personal, so for some time the conversation at lunch centered around financial and domestic complications which appeared to threaten the continued existence of the museum. Eventually, of course, M. Proust's remarks on analogous family situations were cited, and for a short time I felt hovering above me the muses of the great writer and the composer who never met on this earth. The meeting above of these two distinguished ghosts evoked in my mind, irrelevantly enough, the image of the cherubim and seraphim, so often depicted floating toward each other in paintings of the Assumption.

The last time I remember seeing Céleste was several years later, soon after the publication of the second volume of the biography of Proust by George Painter. For reasons I fail to understand, perhaps some latent streak of puritanism, he seemed compelled to prove that, in at least one instance, Proust was bisexual. Had Mr. Painter not scorned the use of unpublished material he would not, I think, have interpreted in so conventional a fashion Proust's *amitié amoureuse* with the not very talented actress Louisa de Mornand. I was curious, therefore, to know Céleste's opinion on the subject.

"Do you remember anything M. Proust said about Louisa de Mornand?" I asked her.

"Yes," she replied. "He said she was stupid."

"Do you think he could ever have gone to bed with her?"

To which question she replied with wonderfully ironic emphasis, *"Anything* is possible, Madame."

Then after a moment's silence she said, "She came to see me a little while ago. She was disturbed by what people told her the English writer had said and I was the only person she thought she could talk to about it."

"What did she look like?" I asked.

"Comme une grosse concierge."

For many years the patterns of our lives diverged to such an extent that I had little news of Céleste. But in 1974, when her book, *Monsieur Proust,* appeared, she sent me a copy with the inscription *"En hommage d'admiration à Madame Mina Curtiss pour qui je garde une profonde amitié et une reconnaissance qui ne disparaitra qu'avec moi-même. Fervente affection. Céleste Albaret."*

Her book contains much that she told me and much that I could have elicited had I been as persistent and imaginative a literary interrogator as the editor who tape-recorded her recollections. One element in the work did surprise me — Céleste's exact quotations from *A la recherche du temps perdu*. She so frequently stated with great humility that she lacked the education to enable her to read M. Proust's work but that he had read her his descriptions of her and her sister.

Touched by the memories her inscription kindled in me and curious about this new Céleste, *femme de lettres,* I asked Liliane, my former research assistant and long-time friend, to pay her a visit and to send me her impressions.

"She is now at Méré, two kilometers from Montfort-l'Amaury," Liliane wrote. "She lives in a brand-new attractive villa with a big garden. The house was built by Odile, who occupies the first floor, while her mother and her aunt have the *rez-de-chaussée*. Céleste has grown very thin. She does not look badly although she explained that last October she had had a slight stroke. She spoke of you with great feeling, tears in her eyes . . . She asked me to tell you that next to Proust you are the person whom she has cherished most in her life and that her admiration for you knows no bounds.

"When I think now of Céleste in the rue des Cannettes and see her in this luxurious house, I am absolutely stupefied."

The page on which Proust wrote the inscription I used in the dedication of my book is reproduced with her youthful photograph on the back cover of her book. Now, in our own equally unpredictable *temps retrouvé,* I would like to echo his words by quoting the dedication I wrote thirty years ago:

> To Céleste Albaret, whom Marcel Proust addressed in 1921 as "*ma fidèle amie de huit années, mais en réalité si unie à ma pensée que je dirai plus vrai en l'appelant mon amie de toujours, ne pouvant plus imaginer que je ne l'ai pas toujours connue.*"

This translation is dedicated in tribute to her devotion to her master's memory, a devotion as loyal, as selfless during the quarter of a century since his death, as was her service to him in the last decade of his lifetime.

Chapter 15

IN MID-MARCH 1952 I wrote to my mother in a state of euphoria. The writing paper was Antoine's, elegantly embossed with a drawing of his house at 45 Quai de Bourbon on the prow of the Ile St.-Louis.

It is so rare that something turns out to be as wonderful as you thought it would be . . . The view is so lovely. I don't know how I shall ever tear myself away from the apartment or get any work done. The barges going by on the river on both sides of the island, the people strolling on the bordering *quai*, the children and the dogs in an enchanting procession. Now, at dusk, with the lights reflected in the water and the Tour St.-Jacques outlined in the sky the outlook is magical. I was much too excited to sleep last night and kept getting up to look out the window. The quiet is unbelievable, only the bells of Notre-Dame tolling the hour. I walk out my door, cross a little bridge and step into the Notre-Dame gardens where flowers are already in bloom and the lawns green. I went for long walks yesterday and today along the *quais,* all so lively and exciting. No tourists at all in this part of Paris, and when I went up to the other part of the city today to order a hat or two I already felt like a visitor.

The apartment I adore as I always have. It is very shabby but comfortable and full of beautiful things. The Vuillard panels are like an interior garden. On my bed are the finest linen sheets, worn and mended, but bordered in wide bands of Venetian lace and embroidered with the princely coronet. The maid is angelic and does everything. She looked after Antoine during his last illness and adored him . . . Having been here just twenty-four hours I feel as though I had been here always. The Ritz seems another life-time.

As I look back now on the happy spring I spent in Antoine's apartment it seems a fitting next-to-last chapter to our very special relationship, one which I know he would have liked. The final chapter, the role he plays in this book, he might not altogether have approved. But it would have amused him.

Antoine died early in September 1951. I had seen him very little the previous year and a half as my visits to Paris were short and he was often away. But his death came as a shock. His mention of dying in the few letters he wrote me during that period I had not taken seriously: "I have again been slightly ill and each time I am sick I say to myself that I am about to die. It is excessively interesting." This note came soon after my return home in the spring of 1949. In 1950 there were two brief notes. One enclosed the script of a radio talk about Proust in which he spoke of my book. "I hope you like it," he wrote. And then "Another train of thought: fruit trees give a maximum crop the year of their death." His collection of Proust's letters had just been published and he had started writing his memoirs, a copy of the first eight pages of which he sent me. (Were there ever any more?) His last letter came from the St. James's Club in London: "This will be the year of my death but I must send you my love beforehand, perhaps today." And then a postscript, "I am going by air today."

The news of his death came to me in the form of an obituary notice, cut from *The Times* of London, sent by my cousin, who wrote on the clipping, "Thought this would interest you." Indeed, as Antoine wrote of his premonition of death, I found it "excessively interesting." I was astonished at the immediate intensity of my reaction. The mail came while I was eating breakfast in bed, so the tears I shed as I read the article inevitably fell into the teacup. My surprise at the sharpness of my emotion over Antoine's death restored my equilibrium so I couldn't help laughing when I thought how pleased he would have been that the announcement of this important event in his life should have found me in bed.

The author of the obituary, Enid Bagnold, the well-known playwright whose *National Velvet* launched Elizabeth Taylor's career, was, he had often said, his oldest, dearest and most generous friend. But he never revealed any of the details of their long-standing relationship. "Prince Antoine Bibesco," the article stated, "who has just died in Paris was nearly forty years my friend. I saw him in London in May and he said: 'I think I shall be dead this year.' That was his joke which he had made before. But all the same he changed his parlourmaid whom he did not like, that she should not be at his deathbed.

"Immensely intelligent . . . he was so private a man that . . . if he could not be intimate he wanted no other relationship. Anything unintimate made him yawn . . . Unique, mocking, staccato, affectionate and impatient, swept by sudden depression and as sudden laughter (against life or himself) he would sit in these last years quite unchanged in his wisdom to his few old friends, in the tarnished silver quiet of his house by the Seine . . . He was extremely vintage, but the ghostly cellar of a man's mind fades, and in the end how we are looked on by our friends is all we have."

Impulsively I wrote to Enid that same day asking her for the details of Antoine's death. As soon as the letter was posted I blamed myself for behaving like an idiot. What sort of reply to an emotional appeal could I expect from an unknown English lady whose privacy I was invading? Certainly not the one I received. For Enid is one of the warmest, most outgoing of women. Four single-space, small-type pages she wrote me — about herself, her family, and Antoine:

The "story" of Antoine's dying is this. He wasn't well in May. He said, laughing, "Well, whatever else it is, it isn't cancer." It *was* a sort of joke; and he really believed he was all right fundamentally, but he had wandering pains and discomforts and was indignant that the doctors couldn't put their fingers on the cause. The next I heard was that he had been ill in Paris and Priscilla had been sent for . . . It was first said that he had cancer of the liver, and then by another doctor that it was only an abscess and not malignant. But the wonderful thing is that he himself never heard the word, *had no pain,* sank, grew so that he didn't remember much what happened the day before, talked little, but said to a friend, "I am losing my memory, little by little — you see — I am even forgetting to die." But he died absolutely peacefully, unconscious and just stopping. So that was great luck.

In another part of her letter Enid asked, "Did you 'love' Antoine? I oughtn't to ask (except that at our age one asks anything — I gather you are fifty-five? — I am sixty-one.) But no one 'loved' Antoine for long. He was too uncomfortable as a lover. As a loved inmate of the heart he settled forever. At twenty-four I used to pray, 'Please God let him marry me.' But I'm glad he didn't. I couldn't have lived next to his darkness and light . . ."

Enid and I met twice — once in New York where she had come for the rehearsals of her charming play *The Chalk Garden*. Later in Paris she came to dine with me in Antoine's apartment, where she had been a familiar for so many years, I only a recent arrival. Although he never liked to introduce his friends to each other this particular meeting with its nostalgic evocations of past relationships did, I think, gain his ghost's approval. As I remember the evening, it seems an ideal donnée for a Henry James story.

2

It was through the kindness of Antoine's daughter, Priscilla, that I was able to live in her father's apartment while his estate was being settled. Quite apart from the aesthetic pleasure of living there, it had the advantage of being only fifteen minutes' walk from my place of work, and what a unique place to work that was.

To get there I walked each day along the Quai aux Fleurs, lingering through the four-block-long flower market and on past the Conciergerie to M. Daniel Halévy's house in the Quai de l'Horloge. There I worked on a little table in the salon, which seemed smaller than it was because of the rows of little chairs that lived there. On the walls were Fragonard and Watteau drawings, on the mantelpiece family miniatures. Out the window the barges chugged up and down the Seine. Across the river loomed the bulk of La Samaritaine department store, a view very different from that of the Quai de Bourbon, but one which I remember with equal warmth. Through several seasons I gazed at it when I would get up to stretch my legs between bouts of reading and copying passages from the diary and letters of Ludovic Halévy, Daniel's father, co-librettist with Henri Meilhac of the opera *Carmen*.

Permission to use his father's archives was only part of the help M. Halévy gave me in my research for a biography of Georges Bizet. He himself was a Wagnerian, a passionate pilgrim to Bayreuth, even in his eighties. He listened unyielding to my protestations against the neglect of Berlioz in France. Neither had he any great taste for Bizet's music nor much interest in him as a man. Nevertheless, he gave me free access to all the archives of his branch of the family, many that he had never read himself but which complemented many of his uncle's and Bizet's documents in my possession.

For six weeks that spring the working conditions were ideal. But the following winter I was forcibly reminded of those postwar years when I was always in a state of chill. There was no central heating in the house. A tiny wood-gobbling stove with a tendency to smoke was supposed to warm the salon. M. Halévy came in each morning, sometimes in his dressing gown, bringing wood to start the fire while I stayed wrapped in woolen underwear, stockings, and my precious fur-lined coat. My feet were partially warmed by a small fur hearth rug which Mme. Halévy brought me the first day. Absorbed though I was in my work, my fingers would eventually protest and grow so stiff I could no longer copy. But in spite of the cold and the smoke, which sometimes forced me to open the window wide, I was in a scholar's paradise.

Often M. Halévy would stop by around noon to see how I was progressing. One day I remember specially he said to me, "I can't understand why a person as young as you should be so absorbed in the past." (He was at the time reading a book by a friend, Hippolyte Taine's niece, about the destruction of Oradour, the French Lidice.) "The present is so much more interesting . . . What, for instance, are you copying out now?"

"A letter from your Uncle Fromental."

"Well, tell me about him," he said. "What was he like?"

"But surely you've read Sainte-Beuve's essay on him?"

"No. What did he say?"

"Well, he said that your uncle was like a bee who never seemed to have found his way into the right hive. If you sat next to him at dinner he never talked about music but about some special subject that had suddenly enthralled him. If he read a book on military history he would decide that he should have been a general. Or a new book on geology would make him think he should have been a scientist. When people were surprised that he continued to hold his position as stage director at the Opéra after the success of *La Juive* he said, 'But a man can't write operas all day long.' I don't think he was ever quite reconciled to being a musician."

"*Un raté comme moi!*" was M. Halévy's comment.

No one could have been less ineffectual than M. Halévy. But his insatiable curiosity about everything to do with the humanities and human experience did sometimes lead him into domains far afield from his political and historical writing. (His *La Fin des notables, La République des ducs,* and his biography of Proud'hon never achieved the lasting recognition of his brother Elie's *History of England in the 19th Century*.) One example of his breadth of interest verged, I thought, on the eccentric.

It was revealed to me when I arrived for tea one day and found all the little chairs in the salon occupied by an extra-ordinary-looking group of gentlemen. (Mme. Halévy and I were the only women.) At first glance I felt as though I had wandered into one of those large group paintings by Fantin-Latour — *Hommage à Delacroix* perhaps. But the men were almost all elderly or old, and the homage was to the 6th Earl of Derby, author of the works of William Shakespeare in the opinion of the majority of those present.

The guest of honor was Abel LeFranc, aged eighty-eight, a tall, handsome man with a long white beard and a splendid head of white hair. In his forties M. LeFranc had been the outstanding world-scholar on Rabelais. But as a result of becoming convinced in middle age of Lord Derby's unrecognized genius, he devoted his remaining half century to spreading this doctrine. Among the other Derbyites were a small, huffy, very aged and aggressive admiral, a member of the Académie Française, and Professor Louis Cazamian of the Sorbonne, author of *Histoire de la Littérature Anglaise,* who may perhaps have been merely a potential convert.

The meeting opened with a little speech by M. Halévy, who wore a high-necked, double-breasted navy blue jacket with a flowing black tie. His beard and long hair had been smartly trimmed for the occasion. His friend Degas would have found him an admirable subject for a portrait. After a brief tribute to M. LeFranc he explained that the meeting had been called because the success of the Comtesse de Chambrun's latest work on Shakespeare had caused the Derbyites to feel that some action was indicated to advance their cause. Methods of propaganda were discussed, the "Stratfordites" being frequently referred to as the enemy. My ignorance of the life of the 6th Earl of Derby, combined with the conspiratorial atmosphere, not unlike the meeting of an undergraduate secret society, tended to give me a sense of confused inadequacy. During the interval, when Mme. Halévy served the only really good tea I ever had in Paris, I approached a rosy-faced young man who had arrived late.

"I suppose you understand all about this," I said.

"On the contrary, Madame. I made an appointment a month ago to ask M. Halévy about Léon Blum. You know he went to school with him. Blum is the subject of my doctoral dissertation."

Wide and unpredictable as were the fields into which M. Halévy's active curiosity led him — I never did find out how or when Lord Derby entered his life — Léon Blum or any distinguished political figure was far more relevant to his basic interest. To my considerable embarrassment I once forgot this fact. When I returned to Paris in the autumn of 1952, M. Halévy, who always omitted preliminaries and small talk, greeted me with, "Tell me about Stevenson." The Stevenson who came first to my mind was Robert Louis. Remembering the French cult for Poe, still active, and more or less incomprehensible to most Americans, I thought that perhaps some French *littérateur* had recently discovered *Treasure Island* or *A Child's Garden of Verses*.

"It's a long time since I have read any Stevenson," I hazarded.

"*Mais non, Madame*. Adlai Stevenson, the candidate for President. You live too much in the past."

There were certain elements of the past, however, that he thought I neglected. He was shocked when he discovered that I had never seen the Basilique de St.-Denis. I explained that I had looked it up in the *Guide Bleu* and after discovering how many times it had been demolished and reconstructed I decided it was a landmark I could miss; that although I admired the good intentions of Viollet-le-Duc, their execution more frequently than not seemed to me aesthetically disturbing. "You are too thorough, Madame, too thorough." (This was a comment with which he often teased me.) I must see the monuments of the Kings of France, he said, and he would guide me. It was a highly adventurous expedition.

At this time M. Halévy's eyesight was already very much impaired. He could see straight ahead but not to either side. In the walks which he continued as long as possible, he carried the white cane of the blind but he crossed streets as though the traffic lights were nonexistent. We went to St.-Denis in an open car, and whereas the friend who was driving us found the traffic almost unbearable, M. Halévy was enchanted by everything he saw, pointing out landmarks he remembered from the days when he had spent much time in that *quartier*. It was there at the turn of the century that he and a group of other intellectual young men had started the Université Populaire, an experiment in adult education which greatly influenced his thinking throughout his life. When we arrived at the church he climbed the stairs so fast that I could barely keep up with him. Inside a guide was conducting a group of tourists whom we joined. But

M. Halévy, not satisfied with the guide's limited spiel, added his own comments, much to the satisfaction of the visitors, who proceeded to follow him rather than the guide. In some miraculous way M. Halévy never stumbled over the many levels in the church. But my anxiety that he might fall so dimmed my capacity either to listen or to observe the monuments of the Kings of France that all I remember is a large expanse of grim ugliness. The beauty lay in the wonderful richness of his mind, his interest and enthusiasm at the age of eighty, and above all in his superb ignoring of any physical danger.

Six years later when he could no longer see to read, he dictated a letter of thanks for the copy of *Bizet and His World* that I sent him. "I am very happy to have your fine book," he said. "I ran my fingers over your immense work and then called my daughter to read me the passages that interested me most. First, Bizet's death, and I do thank you for the tact with which you used my father's notes . . . I remember that we read them together and suspected that several lines hinted of intimate feelings which revealed nothing of importance about Bizet's life." He referred here to the presence in the house at the time of Bizet's fatal illness and death of a friend who might have been, but probably was not, his wife's lover.

In concluding his letter M. Halévy said, "For a worker such as you, this masterly book is by now only a memory, and I already dream of your next book about Manet." (It was never written.)

This remark seemed as right then as it does now. For after writing three other books I am always surprised at what seems new to me when I am forced to look back into the Bizet book to search for the answers to correspondents' questions. I feel as though some other person had written it. Indeed without M. Halévy's cooperation, his continued interest; without the musical instruction, the never-failing day-to-day collaboration of my dear, now dead, friend, the composer Marc Blitzstein; without the generous aid of Winton Dean, Bizet's earlier biographer, I doubt whether there would have been a book worth remembering. In any case one might suppose that the volume M. Halévy honored me by describing as "an immense work . . . a fine masterly book" was the reason for my being awarded the only official honor I have ever received. But that would be a false assumption. For the stepchild of the original handsome hardbound version of *Bizet and His World* that the French publishers chose to produce bore little evidence of the ten years of labor it took to organize the Bizet-Halévy-Straus papers into a scholarly, even readable book. A colorless translation of the text, a third of which, along with all fifty pages of previously unavailable bibliographical material, had been obliterated, would hardly have attracted the attention of many knowledgeable readers or writers.

Epilogue

AFTER THE PUBLICATION of the American edition of *Bizet and His World* I returned to France, taking with me the Sibilat collection, which with the exception of three items I presented to the Bibliothèque Nationale. The manuscript of the "*Habanera*" and Bizet's own copy of the piano reduction of the score of *Carmen* I gave to the Music Division of the Library of Congress, the staff of which had been so generously helpful to me. As a souvenir of the ten years I spent in Bizet's world I kept the Nadar photograph of Rossini, inscribed to the young composer the day before he left for the French Academy in Rome. This delightfully evocative picture is not the only tangible reward for my labors. The little red ribbon I am privileged to wear symbolizes an honor which, deserved or not, I find gratifying.

On a very hot day in June 1960, I was made a Knight of the Legion of Honor in a ceremony at the French Cultural Embassy in New York. Quite apart from its official aspect the day had a highly crucial significance for me. I had emerged from a three months' stay in the hospital only a week or so earlier and was in that state of convalescence when one's legs feel borrowed from an owner who may at any moment reclaim them. Postponement of the ceremony was nevertheless out of the question. I just hoped that if I collapsed as the medal was presented I would gracefully faint into the arms of the official honoring me. That person, to my surprise and delight, turned out to be a close friend whose knowledge of my capacity for coping with crises was in itself reassuring. My immediate impulse was to fling my arms around his neck and say, "Thank God you are here." Quickly enough, however, I realized that he was not present in his identity as my old friend, the poet Saint-John Perse. It was his other persona, that of Alexis Léger, former Permanent Secretary of Foreign Affairs at the Quai d'Orsay with the permanent rank of Ambassadeur de France, Grand Officer of the Legion of Honor, who had come to New York from his home in Washington. He addressed me in these words:

> M. Morot-Sir [French cultural attaché] has very well expressed Mina Curtiss' official rights to the distinction France has conferred on her.
>
> I could, in addition, testify to the interest expressed in Paris literary circles which I myself saw during the circulation of the list of signatures required for the award of this decoration. These signatures were spontaneously given without Mrs. Curtiss' knowledge.
>
> I could evoke the thoughts of friends like Daniel Halévy, André Maurois, Julien Cain, and many others who greatly regret their inability to be here with us for this little ceremony.
>
> I wish, however, more simply, on a more personal level, to claim the privilege of a long-standing friendship, to say only this: In Mina Curtiss I have always recognized a faithful friend of French thought. She bears within herself the essence of France, intimately and familiarly enough to make her a member of the family of France — historic or literary, past or present — like a Frenchwoman born.

Here is the way high French culture has always moved — unpretentiously, from the heart and soul as much as from the mind.

Dear Mrs. Curtiss, permit me to embrace you as a fellow *légionnaire*.

And he kissed me on both cheeks.

Now, after seventeen years, as I translate these words rather awkwardly I realize that at the time Alexis pronounced this little oration it went literally in one ear and out the other, leaving no imprint on my bedazzled, befuddled brain. Today the formality, the flattery rather appall me. For I can't remember ever having felt like a member of the French family. Rather I was an infatuated outsider whose work fortunately enabled her to carry on an enduring love affair with Paris, with the French people and their land. No sense of disloyalty therefore disturbs me at having two years later fallen into a more complex entanglement with quite another sort of civilization.

An account of my love-hate, somewhat irrational passion for Russia — "Mother Russia" — would be out of place in this book. Suffice it to say that in 1962 I went to the Soviet Union with my brother, director of the New York City Ballet, the first American company to perform in the Bolshoi Theatre. Moscow I hated, and left as soon as possible for Leningrad.

This city, though only partially recovered from its hideous wartime siege, bowled me over by its spaciousness, the singularity and variety of its architecture. Only Paris and Venice seemed comparably beautiful. But I was as familiar with the history of those cities as I was ignorant of pre-Soviet Russian history. I did know that Peter the Great created St. Petersburg, and the more I saw of the city and its surroundings the more acute my curiosity about him became. It led me to write my only biography that grew, not out of letters, but out of the impact of architecture, beauty, history. Nevertheless, letters became the basic source of my education in eighteenth- and early nineteenth-century Russian life.

In Washington, where I spent the next two winters, I read in the Library of Congress nearly all of the letters and diaries written by French, German, and English visitors to Russia, starting with Hakluyt down through the 1930s. Consistently enough, out of all this mass of material my hitherto inextinguishable passion for unpublished documents led me into a reckless venture.

Ignorant of the Russian language, dependent on a brilliant but neurotic Russian research assistant, I spent several years exploring and writing the life of a little-known niece of Peter the Great who ruled for only a decade after his death. My choice, however, was not as eccentric as it sounds. The Empress Anna Ivanovna, the subject of my book, introduced opera and ballet to the Russian court and was responsible for founding the first Russian ballet school. For me ballet is a family addiction. And if my explorations into its Russian origins have not been of as much interest to the general reader as they were to me, I at least have the satisfaction of praise from the master.

"When I was in the Imperial Ballet School," George Balanchine wrote me, "I was taught all, or nearly 'all' about Ivan the Terrible, Peter the Great, Catherine the Great and even Alexander the Liberator, but I never even heard about Anna. You have made an unknown Empress live again. It is she who is responsible, of course, for bringing our art of ballet to benighted Russia; it was she more than Peter or Catherine who really 'opened the windows onto the West.' "

Writing *A Forgotten Empress: Anna Ivanovna, 1730–1740* led me into a field of correspondence the very existence of which I had never considered: diplomatic despatches in the Public Record Office in London — fascinating, often decoded communications from the English Resident in Petersburg to his Minister in London. Far more basic, however, was the huge collection of nineteenth-century Russian source material in the New York

Public Library whose officials had the foresight to purchase this treasure in the thirties when the Soviet Union needed cash — an unpublicized expenditure. It is as valuable a contribution to scholarship as Mr. Mellon's acquisition of Rembrandts and Van Dycks was to the arts.

The reader may well wonder why nineteenth-century documents were essential to the biography of an empress who died in 1740 and why one didn't do research in the Soviet Union. The answer is simple. From the time of her death, when she was succeeded by her cousin, the Empress Elizabeth and her successor, the German-born Catherine the Great, both of whom took credit for many of Anna's innovations, Anna Ivanovna was persona non grata in Russia and remains so to the present day. Historically she was treated as an unperson until a century after her death, when the records of her reign became available. The 1840s, however, were prejudicial to any detached account of a Westernizing monarch. And as niece of Peter the Great she was dedicated to continuing his innovations, aided and abetted by her very able ministers for foreign affairs and for war, both trained by Peter and both of German birth. German is the key word. For by 1840 the dispute between the Slavophiles and the Westernizers which raged through a large part of the nineteenth century had already begun. The Slavophiles believed in Russia for the Russians, apotheosizing the Russian people. The Westernizers split into Petersburg and Moscow factions, the aim of the latter being the unremitting denunciation of the Slav version of the Russian people as pseudo-people. Facts troubled the historians of neither party. Diluted propaganda was the result, and Anna Ivanovna's reign has retained the label of "the era of the German yoke."

People may well be as surprised at the persistence of these century-old judgments as I was when in 1970 I returned to Leningrad to gather information and illustrations. The Intourist guide, Galena, was obviously assigned to my secretary and me on the first day of our fortnight's stay in Leningrad to ferret out any clues to possible subversive intentions. She was immediately recognizable as a Party member. In her thirties, stylishly dressed, she soon informed us that she had spent four days each in London, Paris, and Rome, as well as a year in India where she was, fortunately for us, returning the following day as the leader of a group. As we ascended the steps of the State Historical Museum I remarked that I was particularly eager to see the great statue of Anna Ivanovna. "That woman!" she exploded. "She was the cruelest ruler Russia ever had." Resisting the temptation to mention Ivan the Terrible and Stalin, I merely replied that she was responsible for the first ballet school and ballet performances in Russia. "If that is true," Galena said, "someone else in her reign was responsible."

It thus became clear quickly enough that if the authorities learned that my friends, curators at the Hermitage, were cooperating with a foreigner on so taboo a subject their careers might well be jeopardized. So my explanation to them of the subject of my research was the gathering of information for my brother's history of ballet, counting on their ignorance of the fact that it was already published. The day before I left, however, a question from the curator revealed her awareness of the flaw in my excuse. None of the illustrations she had been endlessly helpful in finding bore any relation to ballet. "What is the real subject of your book?" she asked. I didn't answer because I couldn't bear to lie to so intelligent and charming a friend. And it has made me sad to forego the pleasure of sending her my book, the possession of which might risk her security.

Whether my experience in Russia or the days and weeks of struggling to translate into literate language my assistant's basic English version of *Letters of Russian Sovereigns and Other Members of the Imperial Family* revived a lifelong bias against the "Establishment," latent during my years in Paris, I can't say. Certainly in the Soviet Union I encountered the ultimate example. In any case, after using the hard-won material in the biography of Anna Ivanovna my interest in other people's letters waned. And as my eightieth birthday approached I began to wonder about the long-ignored and only vaguely remembered contents of my own letters, some of them kept by my family, others returned by friends at a time when I thought of writing an autobiography.

Reading for the first time since I wrote these spontaneous communications spanning a period of more than half a century it occurred to me that like other people's letters my own had become source material. They made me realize that the period I spent in Paris, crossing the Atlantic Ocean fourteen times in six years, was the most enjoyable of my life both professionally and socially. So it was my own letters that prompted me to write this book.

As I look back now from the perspective of a rather hermetic old age I feel almost as though my Paris adventure of thirty years ago happened to somebody else. Indeed it seems rather as though it had been the fulfillment of one of those adolescent fantasies in which one imagines oneself the center of some romantic yet realistically perceived scene — "the Belle of the Ball," in short. However, my fantasy, inconceivable in adolescence, crystallized only thirty years after it happened. It has left in my mind a permanent magic, reinforced each time I re-read a volume of *A la recherche du temps perdu*. There, rather than in this world in which I am an anachronism, do I feel at home.

Appendix

Notes to Appendix

Index

Appendix

I N THE SUMMER of 1893 one of Marcel Proust's many literary projects was the writing of an epistolary novel in collaboration with Daniel Halévy and Fernand Gregh, his classmates at the Lycée Condorcet, fellow-editors, and contributors to their short-lived, recently deceased magazine *Le Banquet*. The Comte Louis de la Salle, an early friend of Proust's, was the fourth collaborator, and it is only through his letter, reproduced here, that any notion of the plot of this abortive novel is available.

However, Proust's letters in the novel sequence are more significant for their disclosure of the origin of themes that persisted into *Jean Santeuil* and *A la recherche du temps perdu* than for any formulated plan of the work then in hand. His letters are seminal and their long-delayed publication obviously requires an explanation both for professional Proustians and general readers unfamiliar with the vagaries of writers, scholars, and editors. A succession of "ifs" is the keynote to the story.

In 1951, two years after the publication of my translation of Proust's letters, when I was doing research on Bizet at M. Halévy's house, he wandered in one morning to the room where I was working on his father's diary. He handed me a manuscript and said, "This may interest you. I just happened to come across it in a file I had forgotten."

Interested! I glanced at it, recognized Proust's familiar handwriting, suppressed a groan of frustration, and asked permission to borrow the document to read at home. If M. Halévy had kept these fictional letters in the same Proust file as the personal letters he had shown me I could, of course, have included them in my book published in 1949. George Painter in his biography of Proust would perhaps have spared them more than a footnote[1] and Philip Kolb could have placed them in proper chronological order in his edition of the *Correspondance*.[2]

I feel a certain guilt that my procrastination has afflicted the scholarly conscience of my always helpful friend, Professor Kolb. But my lapse in memory responsible for the long delay in publication has, I think, logical justification. At the time that I read and copied the fragment neither M. Halévy nor M. Gregh could remember any participation in the project. If my Bizet research had not wholly plunged me into a pre-Proustian epoch, I might have attempted an explication of the text. But my preoccupation with Bizet's early compositions, his unsuccessful struggles with opera-directors, the complexities of his personal life precluded my stealing the time to read the Proust fragment carefully enough to discern its seminal significance. I filed it away with the rest of my Proust sources.

If after *Bizet and His World* finally appeared in 1958, a visit to Russia had not more or less catapulted me into ten years of researching and writing *A Forgotten Empress: Anna Ivanovna, 1730–1740,* I might, before the centennial of his birth in 1971, have rediscovered Proust's brief experiment. That year I emerged from my inundation in Russian history to resent the almost complete neglect, at least in the United States, of this important anniversary. I wondered therefore whether I might not discover some publishable material in the file ignored for so many years. To my delight I found the fragment, translated it, and offered it to *The New York Review of Books.* An editor came to see me, expressed enthusiastic interest in the work, and asked me to send in a copy of the letters. I requested a prompt decision, as the typescript I was submitting would require revisions in the translation and an explication of the text, while the anniversary year was nearing its end. After several months of editorial silence I received a courteous reply to my written request for a decision or a return of the manuscript. The delay had been caused, it seemed, by the absence abroad of their Proust expert. On his return I would hear from them. Whether he ever returned from abroad I have no way of knowing, for that copy of my transcript disappeared into the for me silent limbo of that impenetrable political-literary stronghold. Another "if" which brings me back to Proust and his story.

Of the eight letters here presented four are written in Proust's own persona to his collaborator, Daniel Halévy, four in the role he assigned himself, the heroine Pauline, to M. Halévy as the Abbé. M. Gregh played himself, the poet, and Louis de la Salle, cast as an army officer, was actually doing his military service that summer.

The casting of Daniel in the role of an abbé puzzled me. In none of his published writings nor in his personality was there any hint of even a brief impulse toward a religious vocation. At first I thought the idea might have been suggested by the charming Abbé Mugnier. But as he became vicar of the fashionable church of Ste.-Clotilde in Paris only three years later it seems possible that Proust's notion of including a priest in his cast of characters may have derived from a personal experience.

In the summer of 1893 he briefly courted a Mlle. Germaine Giraudeau, a relative by marriage to his friend Pierre Lavallée. She sent Proust her photograph after he had drawn a sketch of her in her autograph album with an inscription expressing intimate enough personal emotion to cause her confessor to make her destroy part of it.[3]

Proust may well have cast himself as the lovelorn heroine in a kind of wishful identification with his inamorata of the moment. In another epistolary novel written in collaboration with Comte Robert de Flers, published three years later, the latter was the heroine, Françoise de Breyves, while Proust chose the role of Bernard d'Algouvres, a man of the world.

Readers of *La recherche* are familiar with Proust's intense interest in the significance, the potential appeal to the imagination, of names both of places and of people. The following letters to M. Halévy illustrate his early preoccupation with the importance of names as well as his yet undeveloped range of choice. For these same names appear not only in *"Mélancolique villégiature de Madame de Breyves,"* the story mentioned by Proust, but also in *"Un diner en ville"* and *"La Fin de la jalousie,"* all included in *Les Plaisirs et les jours,* first published in 1896 and republished in 1924 by Gallimard in an edition Proust himself had edited.

The lists, both real and imaginary, that Proust made in his 1908 notebook in which the name Guermantes first appeared, show how much this interest had intensified by the time he started writing *La recherche*.[4]

In his essay *"Journée de lecture,"* published in *Le Figaro* in 1907, Proust makes an amusing comment on his romantic feeling about names. "Doubtless the medieval origin suggested by their names often fails to hold up in association with those who bear them who have neither retained nor understood their poetry. But can one reasonably ask people to appear worthy of their names when the most beautiful things often fail to live up to theirs; when one can't see a country, a city, a river which doesn't diminish the intensity of the dream that its name has kindled? It would be wise to substitute for all social relations, for many journeys the Almanach de Gotha and railroad time-tables."[5]

Proust's absorption in names is apparent in this series of letters, the translation of which has adhered as closely as possible to the

text except for punctuation and paragraphing, which in the
original are either lacking or inconsistent.

Monsieur Daniel Halévy   Postmark July 2 1, '93
2 2 rue de Douai
Paris

Mon cher Daniel,
  Here is the reply. I am charmed by your vivacity as
an abbé. You have immediately hit on just the right
tone. I am annoyed that L. de la Salle has told about my
love affairs. It does simplify things for me, but it would
be better if that were revealed in the very letter that I
shall write to inform him. There is a lieutenant. That's
all wrong because he couldn't send a non-commissioned
officer to deliver a letter to me. I am all admiration. I
shall not say one good thing about him in the whole
novel and while aware of the information useful for my
adventure I shall act as though I attached no importance
to it. It will leak out in spite of me and you will not be
fooled by this but will be tactful enough not to mention
it to me. I replied to him at once. Let's continue this
way. But of course we will arrange the order later so that
no reply ever follows a letter. Later I shall change the
Princesse d'Alériouvre in a short story I have just finished.[6] Madame de Brayves [sic] is already *née* d'Alériouvre. This could be disagreeably embarrassing for
Madame de Brayves [sic].
                    ton ami bien devoué
                    Marcel Proust

Write me to 9 bd. Malesherbes until Monday morning
or even later with a please forward if you have not heard
from me. But you know that apart from one or two exceptions the letters must be much longer. Yours is very

funny but too short. There must be several pages. What shall I do with your and La Salle's letters? Send them to Gregh? But what about Baignères[7] who is to comment on them at Claren. It's confusing. So tell me what to do.

Monsieur Daniel Halévy   Postmark July 21, '93
22 rue de Douai
Paris

                This same Thursday 5 o'clock
Cher ami,
    I am very worried because I am afraid that your exquisite "Vicomtesse de Dives — *née* de Dreux" will *no longer work.* Even admitting that I sign that way sometimes.
    Pauline, sometimes D.D., sometimes a pet name that you will give me, but sometimes I would have to sign Dreux-Dives. But that sounds rather like a railroad line and I am afraid that it will be like that song where Labiche said that if she called herself Bastille she would call her daughter Madeleine because that would come out Madeleine Bastille — nevertheless the thought of renouncing that delicious name upsets me.[8] What shall I do? Reply requested. Sometimes you will have to tease me about my faults so that I can write you some clever, angry letters.

                  Amitiés de t^t coeur
                   Marcel Proust

               9 Boulevard Malesherbes
Cher ami,
    If, as I wrote you in despair this morning, *née* de Dreux will not do because of Dreux-Dives, what do you think of Pauline de Dives, *née* de Gouvre — or *née* de

Guivré or d'Alériouvre or de Frèhel. However, in the *Tout-Paris* there is a M. de Dreux which might be embarrassing for us. As for the signature, it will often be Dreux de Dives which would take away the play on words. I shall find out, or you find out, whether that is as good as signing Dreux-Dives. I think that *née* de Buis or de Buÿ would be very good, too, and even *née* de Buivre, only Buivre-Dives, and perhaps even Buÿ-Dives make too many i's and is too short. For that reason she could be born d'Estranges or d'Aytranges. That doesn't go badly with Dives.

Unless we can interpose temporarily a fifth correspondent I think that La Salle must be the general or at least the colonel in command of my fine young officer. Thus after several letters in which I shall make allusions to unhappy love, to separations, to which you will not reply and which I shall therefore assume that you don't understand, I will ask La Salle to put me in touch with my beloved on a pretext that will not fool him but which will send my lover to me bearing a letter from somebody or other. And you will never know what has happened.

Milles amitiés
Pauline

Although in the previous hastily scrawled note Proust signed himself "Pauline," the body of the letter shows that he had not yet become wholly identified with the heroine. In the following letter he succeeds.

Paris 4 August '93

No I don't forget you, my Abbé, but I would rather not write to you at all than not write *everything*. Since I must reply to you let us again start a correspondence that will both make me happy and do me good. Only you must allow me to leave a part of my heart a blank page. It is all very well to be sincere, but one mustn't be cynical. Besides what would be the use of confessing an intention, the very admission of which transforms it into a definitive reality. In spite of your telling me it is not the priest but the friend, that's even more frightening. There are lots of things that I would tell the priest if I were sure that the friend would forget them.

Divert me. I am very sad and need you very much. The Princesse d'Alériouvre gave an inept performance at her house day before yesterday. I have never seen a claque with so many stupid, vulgar faces. All of Mexico and Uruguay must have been there. There weren't ten people I knew. Nevertheless this party had a certain melancholy charm. It was the last party of the year. You know that it is not for love of people that I ever go out. But think what the last party of the year means. Think of a person (and there are obviously many) who has started to fall in love and who goes to that last party of the year with the feeling that months will go by before she again sees the person she loves. At best, while trying in her misery to reconcile herself to those conditions, she learns that not until winter will she see him again. Just long enough so that she can spend her days and nights at Trouville or St. Moritz, dreaming of Touraine or of Spa. Yes, I pity all the little fragile lives that this preautumnal wind disperses so cruelly that the heart is always far away. It saddens me that this wind is not the afflatus of irresistible sympathies and that their hearts are always so far away. Nevertheless, Abbé, each time it rains, I am sad, remembering the time when as a very little girl I would spend hours at a window to see whether the weather was fair, whether my nurse would take me

to the Champs-Elysées where I played with the little boy
whom I loved as much as I shall ever love in all my life.
The slightest cloud in the sky made me unhappy. A
drop of rain brought tears to my eyes. Each time it rains
I pray for all the lovelorn little girls who cannot go to the
Champs-Elysées and who suffer without anyone's knowing it.[9] Before each ball I pray for those who have no
other opportunity to see the one who is always in their
thoughts, who will be infinitely disappointed if he fails
to come, or those whose mothers decide at the last moment not to go to the ball. Truly the life of a young society girl in love is a poem, and all the more touching
because of its melancholy and suffering. I celebrate the
aftermath of balls like sad anniversaries that have with-
held their promise, particularly the last party of the year.
Also I was too sad, Abbé (without any personal reasons
for being so), at Madame d'Alériouvre's to be as bored as
I should have been, and the horrible people who were
there assume for me a certain grandeur of desolation.
None of this is going to please you, but it is to the friend
I am speaking so that the Abbé will not be annoyed. God
preserve me from becoming a bluestocking. You know
that nothing seems to me so hateful. But I should like
to write some pieces to get rid of my sadness which I
hope will burst like a storm over the sea. But in my present mood you no doubt think that they would turn out
to be tragedies. If you see Chalgrain[10] ask him for some
subjects for me. I have only thought of two and they are
sufficiently tragic. One is about the postmen who trudge
and carry with them so much felicity, so much disappointment. I assure you that for a woman in love the
greatest emotion of each day is waiting for the letters she
expects and even those that she doesn't expect. But even
if she *cannot* receive the letters she longs for because he

who could write them doesn't know she would love to receive them nor even who she is — these very letters she nevertheless waits for; and to reinforce her absurd notions, she turns to all the superstitions, to mysticism, to the oldest romances, to prevent her idea's dying of its very impossibility. Besides it is a daily emotion. For her a meeting in the courtyard with the postman who she knows will not bring what would be so easy for him to carry, is not a trite encounter. But that is not the only side of the subject I shall treat.[11]

All the bad news about sick people, *despatches* to a mother about a mortal accident, hard-hearted letters from a son to his mother, letters from a husband to his wife that build up some irremediable misunderstanding, which no spurts of affection can cure — all this will be in it. My second tragic subject will be the dowagers who spend their time arranging marriages and who sometimes succeed, alas, in their atrocious work of destruction and death. We know some of them don't we, Abbé? You see them doing their needlepoint while discussing their dreadful projects with an air of satisfaction. I shall attempt to develop a portrait of such character that they will seem to be the Fates (are they indeed the Fates?) in the process of weaving our destinies. I think it would have a rather splendid effect to show the *faubourg* salon you know so well, my dear Abbé, suddenly opening and revealing at the back the whole sequence of irretrievable misfortunes that these old women are plotting — the lives steeped in tears; husbands going off with their mistresses, leaving their wives in despair; the suicides, the murders, etc. There, my Abbé, are my fine plans. But I think they are for later, and I even hope, so as not to disgust my friends, and so that Chalgrain will continue to come to see me, that they will never materialize.

I found the articles in the *Gaulois* on Chalgrain's snobbism idiotic. If Chalgrain prefers our society to the other (he is above all an artist) it is like preferring Poitiers or Rome to Chicago or to new industrial cities that have not yet acquired any form or spirit and no recollection of any past. God knows that he makes exceptions for some young Americans (you understand me, Abbé) and neglects certain old Poitiers ladies and austere Romans. Even if I had believed him (although basically he must be pleased with my severity which makes things much more colorful for him) I would have met so many people that in a few years my salon would have become indescribable, something like (oh, horror!) the Princesse d'Alériouvre's.

Tell me whether you will come to spend a month with me, my good Abbé, because then I can perhaps make up my mind to rent a beautiful big place in Touraine where you can hunt to your heart's content. Until now I have just stayed a week at a time, returning to Paris for two or three days which is exquisite: there is no longer anybody there. Do you think I should become involved in the elections this year? Please write me longer letters. I love you with all my heart.

Douvres-Dives

Saint-Moritz

I have been here since yesterday, my dear Abbé, and my departure was so sudden that I couldn't notify you. Even today I only have time to write you. I just want to thank you for your letter which did me a great deal of good. How, like in the photograph album in your salon where I am so much the same at every age, do I continue both in mind and character to be just the way I was, since even as a small child you were already so good to me? For me, at this time when I am so confused, so in search of myself without ever finding it, you are a great prop, a small certainty like a base of operations. I was so nervous I could no longer stay in Paris, and not being able to go where I wanted I minded less intensely going farther away, feeling at least more sheltered against mad temptations, with at least a barrier between them and my lack of willpower — a broad span, a long distance to travel. Alas, thus alone, the depressing strangeness I always feel in new surroundings, particularly in a new apartment, even more cruelly in a new bed, has this time become the true bitterness of exile. I hope to adapt myself quickly and to enjoy in this astonishingly Wagnerian country, all lakes the color green of precious stones and above the mountains over which the clouds cast blue shadows like at sea (you know the great spots on the ocean) and all around pine woods, perfect for the descent of the Valkyries or as a place to meet Lohengrin.[12] On the way that takes fourteen hours in a carriage from Coire there stands on a really inaccessible, vertiginous ridge a castle in ruins whose defunct *seigneurs* make me dream a lot. What crimes, what hereditary vices they must have defended from generation to generation against all curiosity, all hatred, all violence, in this eagle's nest. To attack them would have been mad, to see them in spite of themselves, impossible. The grandiose desolation of the violet mountains around them and the intoxication of an absolute solitude must have carried to excess, have poetized, enlarged to infinity their *voluptés,* without lessening their intensity. For you know, Abbé, Baudelaire said, "There are certain sensations the vagueness of which does not exclude their intensity, and none is keener than that of the infinite." What a place for love! I write these last words without any real thought of their meaning. At the same time the sensation is too strong for me and love, like these mountain-peaks, has its own vertigo.

For the time being I cannot think about this director; when I come back I shall do as you wish, father. But is the man as admirable as you say? Or rather shall I not be too far beneath him to be enlightened by his celestial lights now that the always incomplete humility of my heart and spirit is at even lower ebb, now that I am in a state of profound depression. Wouldn't it be better to wait until this crisis is over, until my soul has regained its calm, until this burden is no longer upon me and I shall have risen to the surface, still so low, but beneath which you want to believe there are some divine lights that could be reflected in a little virtue? I shall do everything you tell me. I am your friend and your servant. Open your arms to me that I may weep in them, console myself and rest there and thus revive your

Pauline

You cannot imagine the elytron-like tone of the lake as I write you. It revives in me the desire I told you about the other day to have some peacocks and an opal. But where the peacocks, my dear? I would really like to look at them in winter and if they were at La Haître how could I do it? My little garden in the ruc Barbet de Jouy is really too small and they would keep me from sleeping. Do you think one could ever get used to their screech? I don't know whether you have the *Chef des odeurs sauves* by Robert de Montesquiou. The book is not yet published but there are some de luxe editions.[13] I am asking because it has some marvelous pieces about peacocks. If you don't know them I will copy them out for you. If you have the book look for a piece entitled *Paonnes* and the following *Paon,* the peacock bird is dead, the God Pan has mourned him. It's that one. I hear that your niece d'Alériouvre is expected here. Is it true?

G.D.

St. Moritz

Oh, *mon cher petit Abbé,* you don't like to see me submissive, you would like me to be angry. Your heart "would swell with joy," my dear Abbé, "if I said you were nothing but a fool." Well, your heart can swell. How can you reproach me for seeing Valkyries behind the trees? Where, my poor man, would you see them? And if I stopped seeing them do you think I would continue to love trees? Don't you know the story of the madman who thought he had the Princess of China in a bottle? Someone broke his bottle. From being a madman he became a fool. Do you wish to base virtue on universal cretinism? God's kingdom would be well populated! For myself, father, if you allow it, and even if you don't allow it, I pray God every night to permit me to see Valkyries behind the trees of the Engadine for a long time more, convinced that they are beautiful, innocent creatures, good to behold wherever one can; and far from compelling myself not to look at their martial grace I shall apply myself to discovering whether one can't see them even better when not conjuring them up; for I believe that we must not desiccate our hearts before offering them to God, but must leave him all the mad flowers that will delight him most. I shall also say, dear Abbé, that it is very strange to hear you say that after listening only to confessions of poor peasant girls you have lost your talent as a director. What kind of director wants to lead only choice, interesting souls, who can serve as models for a case in a psychological novel?

"What Christian sentiments, father!" Would you also like to have your women parishioners rich, well-born, beautiful and able to discourse with distinction on love and passion? I shall no longer be docile, I shall no longer be gentle, if I can. It is too silly. We only respect people who offend us. The people to be obeyed in life we recognize by the tough way they talk to us. So much the better for me, *mon petit Abbé*. You know well that I shall stay nice and affectionate because I can't be any other way, and I am just little Pauline who, you always predicted, could do nothing but love. So much the better for me, for if kindness served a purpose, the imbeciles and the wicked who say kindness is merely a tool of ambition might appear to have common sense. If that were true it would be clever to be disagreeable to everybody, with an occasional lull for which they would be so grateful it would seem like a supreme caress. A bad character is a force with which you can't compete. You see I have thoroughly contradicted you, and if I had the time I should also do it for the Judas about whom your sentiments don't seem to me very Christian, either. As for me, I would have more excuses. But for you, who are not obliged to accept embarrassing invitations, it is inexcusable of you not to open your heart to him. The sun is shining. A breeze is rising over the lake. My boat is ready. I leave you to take the fresh air while fishing for trout before dinner. I shall be thinking of you during those exquisite moments and I embrace you.

Gouvres-Dives

Monsier Daniel Halévy   Postmark 22 — VIII, — '93
Haute-Maison   St. Moritz
Sucy-en-Brie
Seine et Oise

Cher ami,
   La Salle has rewritten the letter and is sending it back
to you. No, nothing should be changed in your letter —
and I would rather croak than tell you any more and am
only saying this to give you a reply. I am for several days
at the Pension Veraguth, St. Moritz — H^te Engadine,
Switzerland, where your letter followed me along with
Louis La Salle's. Has Chalgrain written? We certainly
won't put in just one letter at a time. Later we can insert
the reply like in Hervieu's novel.
                    Mille affectueuses pensées de ton
                            Marcel Proust

P.S. La Salle is reading *l'Intrus*[14] and is fascinated.
   I am keeping your letters carefully and beg of you to
do the same with those you have. Even if we do nothing
with this exchange it will be amusing to read from beginning to end.
   La Salle has been generous enough to sacrifice a second
letter to my love affairs. What luck. The first was mediocre in spite of the beautiful sentence at the end. This
one is an exquisite *"chef-d'oeuvre."* He will write to you
because the next one will be a reply to a request I made
for information about the man I love called Givré. He
has answered and will inform you of the contents in a
letter to take the place of the one you knew that was can-
celed that you sent me. If you have any criticism, I
would be grateful for it.

To Daniel Halévy

Cher ami

I have read the first thirty pages of *l'Intrus* which I find fascinating. When I have finished it I shall write to the Abbé. La Salle and I correspond very conscientiously and he can let him know what is lost.

Is Chalgrain as hard-working as we are?

Mille amitiés,
Marcel Proust

Letter from Comte Louis de la Salle
Postmark Evian Sept. ? 1893

Rambouillet, 5 April

Cher Monsieur l'Abbé,

I am about to take a fortnight's leave to go to the races at Deauville where three of my regiment's horses are running, and I am therefore letting you know so that you won't choose that particular time to leave Barfleur, however much you may wish to. It is so long since I have seen you and it would make me so happy to embrace you, to listen to your talk and to drink your cider under the apple trees from which it flows. Unfortunately I could not spend my holiday as I wished because of having casually accepted an official mission at the race-course. But I shall certainly find the time and the opportunity to come and bring you my news and that of the outside world. Don't think that I have reconstructed my universe around the guardhouse stove, nor even that I am returning from a sidereal voyage. But I did see Sévyères Bachaumont last month, and Madame de Dives, our friend (who, in fact, does closely enough resemble a star). And I think you would enjoy talking about them, even if ordinarily you prefer the conversation of fishermen and the sea. Ah, dear *Monsieur l'Abbé*, it would be hard for me to express my admiration for you! Forgive this sudden outburst, which is basically very sincere, but the rather strange expression of which springs from my feeble opinion of myself at the moment. I am not foolish enough to admire you solely because you love the sound of waves and the silence of the sands, but because for fifty years you have followed the straight and narrow path with calm energy, and because if you look back on your past life you must, in spite of your Christian humility, perceive simple and noble reflections. Perhaps you reply that the true life is in the heart, that you, like other men, have known confusion and sin, and that when you close your eyes, you contemplate paths that have been painful ... [*sic*]

As for me, I have never known what I wanted, nor even what I was doing. I have spent the best part of my life imitating others. I even looked for happiness where I was sure not to find it which is why I am often dissatisfied in spite of my rationalizations to convince myself that on the whole my life is delightful. Dear *Monsieur l'Abbé,* don't despise me for my weakness and my faults, don't write to Madame de Dives that for diversion I draw imaginary pictures, *images d'Epinal* with a little church and a good abbé ... [*sic*]

Speaking of Madame de Dives, I can give you a new and excellent account, having recently received a letter from her, dated St. Moritz. The beginning of the letter is a little hard on me, which is my fault. Our dear Pauline, in fact, was charitable and gracious enough to give me a little English pipe-rack and some English chintz to hang in my room, the shabby, military atmosphere of which depressed her. In thanking her suitably and praising the beauty of her gift, I indulged the singular notion of criticizing in a general way the frightful taste of English upholsterers and then of speaking warmly about unfashionable and familiar old things. She replied quite fairly that I was not very kind and that, besides, a modern armchair in fifty years would have as much faded charm, as many precious memories as an old easy chair has today. Should I tell her by then I shall undoubtedly be dead and consequently shan't care? I don't think it is worth the trouble.

You know that even if I love Pauline, you do sometimes reproach me, dear *Monsieur l'Abbé,* for having an uneasy kind of affection for her. I love her too much not to love even her whims, which she expresses with such charm and so freely. But this time I don't think I am mistaken in being frightened by her fantastic mood. But if I am forced to become involved in things that don't concern me, I sincerely beg of you to look after her.

The reason for these ominous predictions? Here it is: I have in my regiment a very insignificant non-commissioned officer, a bad lot, about whom Madame de Dives, in four long pages, asked me for mysterious information. She even asked me in a way to send her this boy during the maneuvers that will be held around La Haître in September. I am perfectly sure that this has nothing to do with a marriage, that this sergeant in no way knows Madame de Dives, and that he could never have seduced even his chambermaid or his cook. So what does all this mean and in what sort of mess is Pauline getting herself mixed up? *Au revoir, cher Monsieur l'Abbé, et milles amitiés de*

votre Milleroy

What sort of man was Louis de la Salle, I asked myself for the first time while translating his letter written in the persona of Milleroy. Hitherto this letter interested me primarily as the only clue to the plot of the proposed novel. But then my curiosity was aroused by the sudden tardy realization that La Salle was the only one of Proust's childhood playmates, fellow-students at the *lycée,* collaborators on *Le Banquet,* who seemed to disappear wholly from his mature life. The penchant for detection of which I warned the reader in the preface to this book led me to try to discover the motivation behind this apparent cessation of a friendship, so uncharacteristic of Proust's principled loyalty to his friends. Clues to the facts of La Salle's life can be plucked from the exhaustive notes of Philip Kolb's edition of Proust's *Lettres retrouvées* (Paris: Plon, 1966). His personality is reflected in the comments of his friends. These sources, however, fail to provide a solution to the puzzle. Nevertheless I have perhaps self-indulgently included in this digression the results of my research, hoping that some reader, less restricted than I am by geographic and geriatric limitations, might be prompted by these sparse details to carry out further detection.

Comte Louis de la Salle, son of an ordnance officer under Napoleon III, grew up during the aftermath of the defeat of France in the war of 1870. The atmosphere of a military household at this time would inevitably have been disturbing; and perhaps the origin of the self-doubt expressed in the Milleroy-La Salle letter originated during what must have been a difficult childhood.

"As for me," he wrote to the Abbé, "I have never known what I wanted, nor even what I was doing. I have spent the best part of my life imitating others. I even looked for happiness where I was sure not to find it which is why I am often dissatisfied in spite of my rationalizations to convince myself that on the whole my life is delightful."

Whatever the ambiguity in La Salle's nature may have been, he started writing when he was young. His first poems appeared in *Le Banquet*; later he published two volumes of verse — *Poésies* and *Impressions de voyage et autres* — as well as two novels,

Le Joueur de songes and *Le Réactionnaire*. About La Salle's *Impressions de voyage*, published in 1906, Proust wrote two years later in his only published letter to La Salle, "What pains me about my favorite poem, 'Elégies,' is the feeling that whereas my own life for the past several years has been frightful, yours too has not been free of sorrow . . . I have found some of your epigrams really delightful, but in general I cannot sympathize greatly with this universally hostile attitude."

The history of this letter, more distant in tone than habitual with Proust, is as inexplicable as are the reasons for the break in their friendship, so close until 1894. In the summer of 1893, Proust had written to Mme. Straus: ". . . I thought of the poems that Louis de la Salle could recite to you . . . You are so knowledgeable even about things that you don't like that you may perhaps already know them. If they are new to you confess again that they are by M. Mallarmé, that they are clear and that their clarity dispels none of their mystery . . ."

A year later he wrote to a friend, ". . . I dined tonight at La Salle's who told his servant to bring me tomorrow all the wonderful flowers that transformed his apartment into a veritable greenhouse . . ."

After that year La Salle's name is never mentioned in Proust's correspondence. In the 1908 letter in which Proust criticized his old friend's poetry, he mentions his ignorance of his address and wonders whether he will ever receive the letter. Apparently he did not, for it was found by Professor Kolb among Proust's papers in the Bibliothèque Nationale in a collection of letters written to various unrelated correspondents. No logical explanation for their juxtaposition exists. But Professor Kolb's notes including the poems by La Salle quoted in Proust's letter throw some light on the tragic aspect of his friend's life.

On April 26, 1899, La Salle married Madeleine de Pierrebourg, daughter of the Baronne de Pierrebourg, a novelist under the pseudonym of Claude Ferval, and hostess of a literary salon centered around her lover, the successful writer Paul Hervieu. The brief duration of the marriage is revealed in the poem *"Elégies,"* published in 1906:

> ...O days forever incomplete!
> Tell me, did they not have their charm!
> I believe you never think of them
> Without a smile — and I without tears.
> . . . .
> Your son plays near you on the lawn,
> Where once you took your own first steps.
> No longer do you regard yourself as the wife
> Of an unhappy man whom you did not love.

Another poem in this volume refers to La Salle's friend Toulouse-Lautrec, a line from which Proust found delightful: *"Ce que nous avons bu ne peut être décrit"* (What we have imbibed is indescribable). Some months after his marriage La Salle acquired, either as a wedding present or by purchase, a sanguine drawing by Lautrec of a blond English barmaid who worked at the Star *café-concert* in Le Havre. The painter, having recently emerged from a long siege of de-alcoholization in a nursing home, was enjoying sailing, one of his and La Salle's favorite pastimes. An account of a shared sailing expedition evokes an amusing picture of La Salle as well as an aspect of his friendship with Lautrec: "Louis de la Salle, a handsome friend of Lautrec's, a sportsman, proud of his muscles and his magnificent mustache, insisted on sailing with him in very poor weather saying how much he loved the sea." Lautrec had promised to paint La Salle's portrait on condition that he shave off his mustache, which drooped miserably when its owner soon became violently seasick. *"Moustache, moustache,"* Lautrec chanted triumphantly. La Salle, however, remained inflexible, and no portrait of him by Lautrec has been recorded. But when the painter encountered "a man who struggled in vain against his destiny, he dubbed him *'Moustache'* " (P. Huisman and M. J. Dortu, *Lautrec by Lautrec,* New York: Viking, 1964).

How much time La Salle spent sailing and drinking with Lautrec during the early years of his marriage (Lautrec died in 1901) there is no way of knowing. But in 1910, after several years of separation and eventual divorce, the Comtesse de la Salle married Proust's close friend of ten years' standing, the Marquis Georges de Lauris.

No mention of La Salle's personal life appears in *L'Age d'or,* a memoir by Fernand Gregh who in spite of provocation never deviated in his loyalty to the friend of his youth. "Only his difficult character prevented full justice being done his poems in his life-time," M. Gregh wrote. Scattered through his recollections we find corroboration of La Salle's already-mentioned love of the sea — his summers spent in houses he rented at Honfleur and Hennequeville. During one visit to the seashore, Gregh joined his host, accustomed to swimming in the icy waters of the Channel, only to be stricken with a frightful chill, which kept the urban poet bedridden during his whole six-day visit. In speaking of the kindness of his host who, he says, never left his bedside, M. Gregh reveals his own compassionate nature. For La Salle, in a poem entitled *"Art Poétique,"* published in the 1906 volume that elicited Proust's remark about the author's "universally hostile attitude," satirized Gregh cruelly. Obviously influenced by Byron's "The Vision of Judgment," but showing far less talent and far more malice, La Salle not only wrote contemptuously of Mallarmé, whom he had formerly admired, but made fun of Gregh both as man and artist, emphasizing his vanity, his social ambitions, and the absence of originality in his verse. Yet Gregh, writing nearly half a century later, included a description of a youthful dinner party socially important to him, at which he as host somehow tactlessly managed to antagonize all of his guests. They departed in more or less silent disapproval

—all except La Salle who "sensed my unhappiness and, connoisseur that he was, complimented me on the excellent dinner."

"Connoisseur" and "difficult character" are the only concrete verbal clues to La Salle's personality in *L'Age d'or*. But Gregh's words are corroborated by Léon Daudet, the Nationalist, anti-Dreyfus journalist, who knew La Salle at the Café Weber, meeting place of the literati of Paris at the turn of the century. "We were young and gay," Daudet writes in his memoirs, *Salons et journeaux* (Paris: Bernard Grasset, 1932). "We lived in happy freedom from care, interrupted by violent rages and justified resentments. I think of Louis de La Salle, a literary man among writers, a subtle observer, often bitter about contemporary society . . . Although he appeared to be a man about town he was highly cultured, widely known, pampered, yet basically inflexible, difficut to cope with in a political discussion." (Since like all members of the *Banquet* group La Salle was a Dreyfusard, the restraint of Daudet's comment here is worth noting.) "La Salle was uncompromisingly patriotic," Daudet continues. "I used to say to him 'You have the soul of a fighter. Don't fool yourself,' and to myself I thought he was by nature a hero."

In October 1915 La Salle sent Daudet a message of sympathy on the death in battle of a fellow-officer, a colleague of the journalist on his reactionary paper, *L'Action française*. He closed his letter with the words "My turn soon," a prophecy which came true only a few days later.

This same year Proust wrote to a friend, "Have I talked to you about all my friends who have been killed in the war? I keep harping on this subject because I think of nothing else." Yet in none of his wartime letters does he mention the death of Louis de La Salle.

Notes to Appendix

1. George D. Painter, *Proust: The Later Years* (Boston: Little, Brown, 1965), p. 26.
2. *Correspondance de Marcel Proust: 1880–1895*, ed. Philip Kolb, (Paris: Plon, 1970).
3. Kolb, Vol. I, p. 212, n. 3.
4. *Cahiers de Marcel Proust*. Nouvelle série 8. *Le Carnet de 1908*. Établi et Présenté par Philip Kolb (Paris: Gallimard, 1976), pp. 111, 115–17.
5. Marcel Proust, *Chroniques* (Paris: Gallimard, 1927), p. 88.
6. *Mélancolique villégiature de Madame de Breyves. Les plaisirs et les jours.* (Paris: Gallimard, 1924). First published in 1896 with a preface by Anatole France, illustrations by Madeleine Lemaire, and four piano pieces by Reynaldo Hahn.
7. Jacques Baignères, a schoolmate of Proust's, whose mother, Mme. Laure Baignères, was a prominent hostess.
8. Labiche's popular song *"Madeleine-Bastille"* sprang from the name of the *"ultra-rapide"* three-horse omnibus line introduced in 1878. Dreux and Dives are French cities. Therefore Dreux-Dives as signature to a letter would be analogous to signing one-self Lynchburg-Danville.

9. "Only, would *she* come again to the Champs-Elysées? Next day she was not there; but I saw her on the following days; I spent all my time revolving round the spot where she was at play with her friends, to such effect that once, when, they found, they were not enough to make up a prisoner's base, she sent one of them to ask me if I cared to complete their side, and from that day I played with her whenever she came. But this did not happen every day ... There were also the days of bad weather on which her governess, afraid, on her own account, of the rain, would not bring Gilberte to the Champs-Elysées.

"And so, if the heavens were doubtful, from early morning I would not cease to interrogate them, observing all the omens. If I saw the lady opposite, just inside her window, putting on her hat, I would say to myself: 'That lady is going out; it must, therefore, be weather in which one can go out. Why should not Gilberte do the same as that lady?' But the day grew dark. My mother said that it might clear again, that one burst of sunshine would be enough, but that more probably it would rain; and if it rained, of what use would it be to go to the Champs-Elysées?" Marcel Proust, *Swann's Way*, tr. C. K. Scott-Moncrieff (New York: Random House, 1934), p. 302. Also see *Jean Santeuil*, tr. Gerard Hopkins (New York: Simon and Schuster, 1956), pp. 46–47.

10. Henry Chalgrain was the pseudonym Fernand Gregh adopted for some of his early poems and for his role in this novel.

11. "And when the time came for the postman I said to myself, that evening as on every other: 'I am going to have a letter from Gilberte, she is going to tell me, at last, that she has never ceased to love me, and to explain to me the mysterious reason by which she has been forced to conceal her love from me until now, to put on the appearance of being able to be happy without seeing me; the reason for which she has assumed the form of the other Gilberte, who is simply a companion.'

"Every evening I would beguile myself into imagining this letter, believing that I was actually reading it, reciting each of its sentences in turn. Suddenly I would stop, in alarm. I had realised that, if I was to receive a letter from Gilberte, it could not, in any case, be this letter, since it was I myself who had just composed it. And from that moment I would strive to keep my thoughts clear of the words which I should have liked her to write to me, from fear lest, by first selecting them myself, I should be excluding just those identical words, — the dearest, the most desired — from the field of possible events. Even if, by an almost impossible coincidence, it had been precisely the letter of my invention that Gilberte had addressed to me of her own accord, recognising my own work in it I should not have had the impression that I was receiving something that had not originated in myself, something real, something new, a happiness external to my mind, independent of my will, a gift indeed from love." *Swann's Way*, p. 312.

"I had just written Gilberte a letter in which I allowed the tempest of my wrath to thunder, not however without throwing her the lifebuoy of a few words disposed as though by accident on the page, by clinging to which my friend might be brought to a reconciliation; a moment later, the wind having changed, they were phrases full of love that I addressed to her, chosen for the sweetness of certain forlorn expressions, those 'nevermores' so touching to those who pen them, so wearisome to her who will have to read them, whether she believe them to be false and translate 'nevermore' by 'this very evening, if you want me,' or believe them to be true and so to be breaking the news to her of one of those final separations which make so little difference to our lives when the other person is one with whom we are not in love." Marcel Proust, *Within a Budding Grove*, tr. C. K. Scott-Moncrieff (New York: Random House, 1934), p. 446. Also see *Jean Santeuil* pp. 53–54.

12. In July 1893 Proust wrote to his friend Pierre Lavallée, "... I am working hard, but go out a little especially to see the *Valkyrie*." The Paris première of *The Valkyrie* took place May 12, 1893. In the original version of *Mélancolique villégiature*, published September 15, 1893, in *La Revue Blanche*, Proust mentioned Act I, Scene 5, of *The Valkyrie*. But he cut this passage from the version in *Les Plaisirs et les jours*. *Correspondance*, I, pp. 226–227.

"I began to perceive how much reality there is in the work of Wagner, when I saw in my mind's eye those insistent, fleeting themes which visit an act, withdraw only to return, and, sometimes distant, drowsy, almost detached, are at other moments, while remaining vague, so pressing and so near, so internal, so organic, so visceral, that one would call them the resumption not so much of a musical motive as of an attack of neuralgia." Marcel Proust, *The Captive*, tr. C. K. Scott-Moncrieff (New York: Random House, 1943), p. 489.

13. On June 25, 1893, in acknowledgment of a pre-publication copy of *Chef des odeurs suaves*, Proust wrote one of his more elaborately flattering letters to his social mentor, the Comte Robert de Montesquiou, who was to become the chief model for the Baron Charlus: "... I am too deeply stirred to be able to compare this book to *Chauves-souris*. But for a subject not susceptible to analysis, because the divine reasoning that permeates it releases it from time, space and personal relations to a purely mysterious level like music or faith, I believe that there are more lines here that foreshadow it, reveal it in bringing it to life... After the fourteen most marvelous lines that you have ever written... there is this divine moment:

> Yeux crevés, paons privés de
> tous leurs luminaires
> Pourtant plus adorés
> Des poètes encor!
> (Eyes dead, peacocks bereft of all their glow,
> Yet more adored
> By poets still!)

It is heart-breaking, one can't say why. To this extent art no longer bears its own explication. Some of Wagner's phrases have this sweetness..." *Correspondance*, I, p. 214.

14. *L'Intrus* by Gabriele d'Annunzio, first published in Italy in 1892 entitled *L'Innocente*, appeared the following year in a French translation serially in *Le Temps*, as well as in book form. In the United States a translation called *The Intruder*, published in 1897, was popular enough to be reprinted four times during the

next decade. In Italy it has apparently never been out of print. In France it introduced the D'Annunzio cult which flourished at varying levels of intensity until the 1914 war.

"Dostoyevskyan" one writer labeled *The Intruder*. A more recent biographer, Philippe Jullian, finds "this tale of adultery" influenced by Maupassant and Tolstoi. But the book is admittedly autobiographical. A glance through its pages of melodramatic hyperbole leaves one with the sensation of having been exposed to a low-grade B Italian film. The intruder, one discovers, is a baby of doubtful origin whose death is caused by the jealous, cuckolded possible father.

It is difficult to understand the fascination of the two aspiring young novelists with a book that today seems a caricature of D'Annunzio, the great lover, describing his methods of seduction. Perhaps the remarks of Proust's friend of a younger generation throw some light on the subject. Maurice Rostand, son of the author of *Cyrano de Bergerac*, writes in his *Confession d'un demi-siècle:* "Gabriele d'Annunzio? I don't know how to express what that name meant to me then. It evoked so many things: madness and Italy, elegance and extravagance, bad taste and genius... Doubtless there are defects in d'Annunzio's writing but in what great work are there not? ... One need only re-read *l'Intrus* to rediscover the fever which spread to everyone..."

An Index of Names

1979 -

Mon cher Daniel

Voici la réponse. Je suis charmé
de ta vivacité d'abbé. Tu as tout de
suite eu le ton le pl. juste. Je suis
ennuyé que D. de la Salle l'. ait
écouté mes amours. Cela me sim-
plifierait les choses. Mais il vaut mieux
que cela se déconne dans la lettre même que je lui écrirai pour le savoir
L'. en ait fait un lieut! c tel tu
mauvais c'st sous off. Σ cet